Timor

WORLD BIBLIOGRAPHICAL SERIES

General Editors:
Robert G. Neville (Executive Editor)
John J. Horton

Robert A. Myers   Ian Wallace
Hans H. Wellisch   Ralph Lee Woodward, Jr.

John J. Horton is Deputy Librarian of the University of Bradford and currently Chairman of its Academic Board of Studies in Social Sciences. He has maintained a longstanding interest in the discipline of area studies and its associated bibliographical problems, with special reference to European Studies. In particular he has published in the field of Icelandic and of Yugoslav studies, including the two relevant volumes in the World Bibliographical Series.

Robert A. Myers is Associate Professor of Anthropology in the Division of Social Sciences and Director of Study Abroad Programs at Alfred University, Alfred, New York. He has studied post-colonial island nations of the Caribbean and has spent two years in Nigeria on a Fulbright Lectureship. His interests include international public health, historical anthropology and developing societies. In addition to *Amerindians of the Lesser Antilles: a bibliography* (1981), *A Resource Guide to Dominica, 1493-1986* (1987) and numerous articles, he has compiled the World Bibliographical Series volumes on *Dominica* (1987), *Nigeria* (1989) and *Ghana* (1991).

Ian Wallace is Professor of German at the University of Bath. A graduate of Oxford in French and German, he also studied in Tübingen, Heidelberg and Lausanne before taking teaching posts at universities in the USA, Scotland and England. He specializes in contemporary German affairs, especially literature and culture, on which he has published numerous articles and books. In 1979 he founded the journal *GDR Monitor*, which he continues to edit under its new title *German Monitor*.

Hans H. Wellisch is Professor emeritus at the College of Library and Information Services, University of Maryland. He was President of the American Society of Indexers and was a member of the International Federation for Documentation. He is the author of numerous articles and several books on indexing and abstracting, and has published *The Conversion of Scripts* and *Indexing and Abstracting: an International Bibliography*. He also contributes frequently to *Journal of the American Society for Information Science*, *The Indexer* and other professional journals.

Ralph Lee Woodward, Jr. is Chairman of the Department of History at Tulane University, New Orleans, where he has been Professor of History since 1970. He is the author of *Central America, a Nation Divided*, 2nd ed. (1985), as well as several monographs and more than sixty scholarly articles on modern Latin America. He has also compiled volumes in the World Bibliographical Series on *Belize* (1980), *Nicaragua* (1983), and *El Salvador* (1988). Dr. Woodward edited the Central American section of the *Research Guide to Central America and the Caribbean* (1985) and is currently editor of the Central American history section of the *Handbook of Latin American Studies*.

VOLUME 142

Timor

Including the islands of Roti and Ndao

Ian Rowland

Compiler

CLIO PRESS

OXFORD, ENGLAND · SANTA BARBARA, CALIFORNIA
DENVER, COLORADO

British Library Cataloguing in Publication Data

Rowland, Ian
Timor. – (World bibliographical series; v.142)
I. Title   II. Series
016.95986

ISBN 1–85109–159–9

Clio Press Ltd.,
55 St. Thomas' Street,
Oxford OX1 1JG, England.

ABC-CLIO,
130 Cremona Drive,
Santa Barbara,
CA 93117, USA.

Designed by Bernard Crossland.
Typeset by Columns Design and Production Services Ltd, Reading, England.
Printed and bound in Great Britain by
Billing and Sons Ltd., Worcester.

THE WORLD BIBLIOGRAPHICAL SERIES

This series, which is principally designed for the English speaker, will eventually cover every country (and many of the world's principal regions), each in a separate volume comprising annotated entries on works dealing with its history, geography, economy and politics; and with its people, their culture, customs, religion and social organization. Attention will also be paid to current living conditions – housing, education, newspapers, clothing, etc.– that are all too often ignored in standard bibliographies; and to those particular aspects relevant to individual countries. Each volume seeks to achieve, by use of careful selectivity and critical assessment of the literature, an expression of the country and an appreciation of its nature and national aspirations, to guide the reader towards an understanding of its importance. The keynote of the series is to provide, in a uniform format, an interpretation of each country that will express its culture, its place in the world, and the qualities and background that make it unique. The views expressed in individual volumes, however, are not necessarily those of the publisher.

VOLUMES IN THE SERIES

For Cathy

Contents

Contents

Contents

Preface

The general aim of the bibliography is to present Timor in all its facets to the English-speaking world. Entries have been selected for their authority, variety and ease of access. The neighbouring islands of Roti and Ndao are also included as they are physically, historically and politically closely related to Timor.

The long period of Timor's colonization and its recent troubled history have given rise to a large body of literature devoted to an island of its size. Those seeking information are faced with numerous limitations and individuals intent upon utilizing this volume as a introduction to forays into the field of Timorese studies should be aware of some caveats. For example, although the majority of references are in English, much historical work has been conducted in Portuguese and Dutch and there is a growing body of work in Indonesian. The range of publications on Timor reflects the dominance of studies on a limited number of subjects, notably anthropology and the Indonesian annexation of East Timor.

Much of the material on Timor is dated, though not necessarily obsolete, and any extensive study of Timor is likely to involve large numbers of semi-published official documents and technical studies, many of which are not readily available in the anglophone world. Despite these limitations it is hoped to introduce readers to the main bibliographical sources which will lead to deeper research.

Classification of some works presents problems in any scheme. The preponderence of works in the 'Timorese Peoples' section demonstrates this most clearly. Anthropology is the widest study of mankind's endeavours and in seeking to classify this material within formalized parameters invariably one is left with a subjective approach to an author's intention. The chapters on oral literature, the arts, and agriculture could easily constitute items about ethnic groups. In these cases, the most likely chapter one might expect to locate such material has been chosen and cross-references have been provided to guide the reader.

Since 1974 the nature of the island's politics has led to isolation from the world press, numerous restrictions on information, and questionable facts and figures. Prior to this, the island's physical remoteness from Lisbon, Amsterdam and Jakarta served to create a similar paucity of information. The Indonesian annexation of East Timor has, however, generated a number of widely available, cheap paperbacks which often contain much background information on the island.

Very few works appearing during this time (apart from technical and scientific ones) do not have marked political biases. A good deal of material has also been produced by human rights organizations, left-wing groups and governments. These sources also carry sometimes severe biases. The inclusion of representative works has meant, in some cases, that items have been listed putting forward arguments that the author cannot possibly support. The issues of truth and falsehood weigh heavily with the reader.

All the works cited are to be found in one or more of the collections in England acknowledged below, and much the same titles are likely to be available in the United States, Australia and elsewhere.

As is the case in all such endeavours, the bibliography builds upon the preliminary archival exploration of scholars and research institutes. Pre-eminent in this field is Kevin Sherlock, to whom my thanks are due for advice and inspiration. His work in the archives of Australia, Lisbon and Macau has paved the way for the study of Timor in all disciplines. More importantly, with the challenges facing indigenous Timorese scholarship, his Timor Collection is currently documenting, summarizing and preserving material on Timor for the Timorese people and other interested persons.

I am also indebted, for facilitating research in London, to the staff and librarians of the School of Oriental and African Studies (University of London) especially Helen Cordell, Ulrich Kratz and Nigel Phillips, the University of London Library (Senate House), British Library of Political and Economic Science, British Library, Royal Geographical Society and the staff of the Catholic Institute for International Relations. Jill Jolliffe, the National Library and the Geographical Society of Lisbon in Portugal and Cliff Morris in Australia very kindly answered my queries. Finally, thanks are due to my sister, Helen Oldcorn, for the use of her word processor.

Introduction

Timor is the largest and most easterly of the Lesser Sunda Islands, or Nusa Tenggara, which stretch out between Bali and Australia.

The island, lying on a southwest-northeast axis, is about 500 kilometres long and 100 kilometres wide. It has a land area of 33,600 square kilometres, similar to that of Taiwan, somewhat larger than Belgium. The nearest landmass is Australia: Darwin lies 800 kilometres to the southeast of Kupang, the island's largest city.

West Timor, covering 19,000 square kilometres, is part of the Indonesian province of Nusa Tenggara Timur. East Timor, under Indonesian administration since 1976, forms the province of Timor Timur and is slightly smaller at 14,600 square kilometres.

Population levels are fairly low. In 1980 West Timor had a population of 1.2 million and East Timor a population of 700,000. Apart from the main urban centre of Kupang, the provincial capital of Nusa Tenggara Timur and the largest city in Nusa Tenggara the population tends to be widely scattered, reflecting the distribution of cultivable land.

Geology

Geologically, Timor is quite young, originating in the late Tertiary and Quaternary periods, some seventy million years ago. Plio-Pleistocene sedimentation was followed by vigorous uplift with the collision of the Sahul plate to the south with the more resistant Sunda plate to the north. The Sunda plate was pushed to the surface, scraping up the coral reefs and marine sediments, folding them intensely and piling them up into parallel ridges.

These sediments are a mixture of folded coral limestones, marls, sandstones and clays. Embedded in the clays are fragments of many different rock types, including fragments broken off the leading edge of the Sunda plate. Timor and Roti are without recent volcanic formations.

Introduction

Soils

These raised coral reefs and sediments, barren limestone plains and sparse savannas on the poor, eroded soils which accompany this geology can, in places, barely support cattle. Limestone, marl and calcareous clay are widespread, with shallow layers of red or brown clayish soils overlying them. Population pressures have led farmers to shorten the crucial fallow period in Timor's traditional slash-and-burn agriculture, putting pressures on soils.

Climate

Timor is one of the driest parts of Indonesia, with an average annual rainfall of less than 1,500 millimetres.

In the main the climate follows the general pattern of the Indonesian archipelago, with temperatures which vary from 18–21°C to 26–32°C, and the year divided into a rainy season and a dry season. But because of the proximity of the Australian land mass, the annual precipitation cycle on Timor is much more sharply defined than in the more westerly parts. It is this marked seasonality that divides the year, controlling agricultural activity and, traditionally, the rhythm of social life.

Despite the general monsoon patterns the rainfall distribution is highly complex and controlled largely by local topography. The highest part of Timor can receive more than 3,000 millimetres of rain each year, whereas coastal or sheltered inland plains receive less than 1,500 millimetres and some parts of north Timor receive between 500–1,000 millimetres. Timor is the only part of Indonesia subjected to tropical cyclones.

At the beginning of the dry season when the harvest has been gathered there is time for other activities, in their turn often determined by the climate. Salt making, felling of sandalwood trees, the collection of beeswax, the island's second export commodity for ages, are all traditionally dry season jobs. The dry season is also the time for building houses and repairing roads, and general relaxation: feasting and dancing, travelling and leisure.

This seasonality is seen at its most profound on the tiny island of Ndao. The island is dry for most of the year, yet the island supports high population densities. Before the southeast monsoon makes entry to the island's only harbour impossible, the men leave to become itinerant silversmiths on the neighbouring islands. They return at the beginning of the wet season to resume tending their gardens. While their husbands are away the women weave *ikat* cloths for the men to sell during the next dry season.

Geography

In many places farmers have to depend on rainfed agriculture, growing corn, cassava and other tuberous crops. Maize was probably introduced into Timor by Europeans in the seventeenth century and, well suited to the ecology of the island, today constitutes the staple of the Timorese diet.

Rice is grown in irrigated paddyfields where possible; in recent years it has been introduced to the river valleys, although in many places it is still largely viewed as a ceremonial food.

The small, arid island of Roti (1,280 square kilometres, maximum elevation 350 metres) lies south-south west of the south coast of Timor and is separated from it by a narrow strait. As with Timor, the economic and social life of the island is greatly affected by the climate. The east monsoon between April and October brings hot, dry weather with gusty winds. From November until January there is usually sporadic rain brought by the western monsoon (average 1,000 millimetres per annum), but this is often late in arriving, causing low yields of maize, sorghum, peas, pumpkins, onions and the various tubers grown in the swidden gardens.

To counter this uncertainty the greater majority of the 100,000 Rotinese supplement their meagre diet during the long dry season with a sweet syrup taken from the inflorescences of the lontar palm (*Borassus sundaicus*). The inflorescences of the palms are tapped and the juice boiled until it becomes syrup. Mixed with water, this syrup provides most of the daily food for the Rotinese.

The produce from the swidden gardens is often used only in feasts and festivals, even millet and maize are used sparingly. By diverting streams and creeks to irrigate the fields the island has become self-sufficent in rice. Fishing also supplements the diet in the long dry season.

In the more rolling grassland areas of Timor (for example, Amarasi in the southwest) cattle husbandry has been introduced with varying levels of success.

The leguminous drought-resistant shrub *lamtoro* (*Leucaena leucocephala*) has been hailed recently as having the potential for bringing promising change in the agricultural potential in this, one of the driest regions of Indonesia. *Lamtoro*, which, like many leguminous crops is able to fix atmospheric nitrogen in the soil, is said to have served on Java and Sumatra since the beginning of the nineteenth century as a shade tree on coffee, kapok, vanilla and coconut plantations and has acted incidentally as a soil fertilizer and as protection against erosion but in Nusa Tenggara Timur has been used in the past mainly for hedges and charcoal. Serious pest attacks and high levels of mimosine in the leaves, a chemical causing hair loss in cattle, have since countered this optimism.

Introduction

Landscape

Its turbulent geological past has left Timor with an impressive topography broadly characterized by a core of mountains rising to 2,920 metres at Tata Mai Lau in the Ramelau range of East Timor and 2,365 metres at Tubu Mutis in West Timor.

In the western half of the island this central mountain chain splits into two mountain ranges that run roughly parallel to the coasts, enclosing a series of highland plateaux. These central highlands contain much of Timor's population in what has become an eroded, almost treeless landscape.

Towards the north coast these mountains generally run straight into the relatively calm Wetar Strait. To the south of the mountain chain lies a broad, fertile plain fringed by the rougher Timor Sea. The coastline is regular, with long stretches of cliff alternating with narrow sandy beaches, guarded by coral reef. Large parts of the coast, particularly at the eastern and western ends of both Timor and Roti, are formed of broad terraces of reef limestone.

Running through this landscape are many short, braided rivers, showing a marked seasonal fluctuation in volume as a result of the regular alternation of dry and wet seasons. In the rainy season they are wide and turbulent, nearly impassable. With the onset of the dry season the rivers gradually decrease in volume and speed and return to narrower, gravelly channels. None of the rivers is navigable and most of them dry up completely at some time during the dry season.

Flora and fauna

Timor's rocky soil and long dry season does not support dramatic vegetation types or a large variety of endemic species. Low scrub is widespread with casuarina (*Casuarina equisetifolia*) and eucalyptus (*Eucalyptus urophylla, E. alba*) at higher elevations. The sandalwood (*Santalum album*) forests which brought fame to the island are now reduced to a few vestigial traces in remote areas of the the island, although the government has recently sponsored efforts to replant trees. The fire- and drought-resistant lontar palm is one of the most useful plants in the region, serving as an important source of nutrition.

These vegetation types support a few large animals: wild deer (*Rusa timorensis*), pigs, monkeys and the various domesticated animals that have been introduced relatively recently by man. In fact, it is likely that all of the larger animals have been introduced during the last 5,000 years or so. There are also rats, bats, lizards and snakes. In contrast to this situation is the marine life around the island, with magnificent reefs home to large numbers of species of fish.

Timor lies to the east of the Wallace Line: its flora and fauna are related more to those of Australia than to those of Asia due to habitat and the obstacles provided by sea crossings. Asian fauna thrive in the western part of the archipelago because of the higher rainfall and tropical forests there, a habitat that matches mainland southeast Asia. In the east, Australial fauna survive because they are adapted to dry, scrubby landscapes.

This transition zone between Asia and Australia is called Wallacea after Alfred Russel Wallace who spent the years between 1854–62 exploring the archipelago. He noticed that the number of Asian species diminished as he moved east, while the number of Australian species increased. He drew a line on a map of the Indonesian archipelago, straight between Borneo and Sulawesi, and Bali and Lombok, known today as the Wallace Line. Wallace reasoned that, during the last glaciation, the seas fell leaving dry land between Bali and Singapore, but not between Bali and Lombok, because of the deep Lombok Strait, which had the effect of stopping plants and animals from moving across.

This theory is now fairly well discredited, mainly on botanical grounds, as the archipelego shows no sharp breaks in the distribution of its 2,300 genera of plants, but in honour of Wallace's ground-breaking biogeographical work the region still carries his name.

Archaeology and prehistory

It is thought that Australoid humans from the west were the first humans to inhabit Timor and, if so, that it is likely that they went on to settle in Australia as well. Excavations in four caves near Baucau and Venilak in East Timor have uncovered a stone tool industry from about 13,000 years ago. The finds include bones and remains of the contemporary native fauna of the region – giant rats, fruit bats, snakes, reptiles, fish and shellfish. Indonesian archaeologists have recently made finds of pre-agricultural archaeological remains in Gua Oelnaik, near Camplong in West Timor.

During the last 5,000 years the whole region has witnessed a gradual influx of predominantly Austronesian peoples, bringing with them agriculture, domesticated animals and skills such as pottery-making. The excavations at Baucau and Venilak have revealed simple pottery, shell beads and bracelets, fragments of shell fishhooks, and bones of pigs beginning about 5,000 years ago. Dog, goat, cattle and water buffalo bones are more recent, 3,000 years old or less.

Bronze and iron, and perhaps the ability to work them, were present in the archipelago by about 2,000 years ago, but the cultural influences of Indian traders that so deeply affected the cultures of Java and Bali were never strong in Nusa Tenggara so Timorese society can be considered to have been essentially prehistoric and Austronesian until the spread of Islam in the fifteenth and sixteenth centuries.

Timorese people

The original inhabitants of Timor are thought to be what are now known as the Atoni (who call themselves Atoni Pah Meto – 'the people of the dry land'). They are still predominant over most of West Timor, inhabiting the slopes of the river valleys in the mountains in the interior. Their economy was traditionally concerned with subsistence agriculture, with maize as the staple crop.

With various waves of invasion over the last 3,000 years the number of ethnolinguistic groups on the island has increased to about eighteen. Most of the languages fall within the Austronesian language family and the languages spoken are closely related to those of the Moluccas. The language of Ndao is more closely related to the languages of the western Lesser Sunda islands.

There are also communities of speakers of non-Austronesian or Papuan languages at the eastern end of, and in one part of central, Timor, with affinities to languages spoken in New Guinea.

For trade and communication, Malay has for centuries served as a lingua franca, and its modern form, Bahasa Indonesia, is the language of government and education throughout the island.

Undoubtedly, one of the most important invading groups was the Tetun who, according to Timorese oral history, arrived from Macassar (modern Ujung Pandang in Sulawesi) and Larantuka, on the eastern tip of the nearby island of Flores in the fourteenth century, displacing the Atoni into the mountains and settling the fertile Benain plain on the south coast of West Timor. The fertile soil of the plain enabled the Tetun to create a powerful kingdom – Wewuki-Wehali – and to this day they are one of the dominant people in the island.

In 1642 Portugal shattered the power of the Wewuki-Wehali kingdom, and it fragmented into two separate alliances loosely arranged along the linguistic boundaries. The Tetun-speaking kingdoms of the eastern part of the island became the Belu empire and those of the west becoming known as the Servião.

This is reflected in the modern distribution of the Tetun ethnolinguistic group. It is found in three main areas – the eastern Tetun in the eastern area around Viqueque in East Timor, and the western and southern Tetun in the western, or Belu, area: a broad corridor running from the north to the south coast and lying on both sides of the border separating East and West Timor.

Modern Timorese society is characterized by a large number of migrants from Roti. The nature of their presence in Timor is interesting and worthy of note. The Rotinese, upon being colonized by the Dutch and attracting the attention of the Christian churches, turned this to their advantage, assimilating the religion well and attaching a certain prestige to education. Their industriousness has enabled Rotinese migrants in their new home of Timor to rise to fairly high levels of government, church, and education.

The concept of complementary duality is one which underlies much of traditional Timorese life, and is central to understanding events in Timor in the historical sense, and also for understanding Timorese religion and society even today. Many things, both concrete and abstract are classified in complementary pairs: male/female, black/white, inside/outside, for example. People orientate themselves by referring to the mountains and the sea, in a social context people are younger and older, for example. The ritual language used to address gods and ancestors also uses twin groupings of parallel sentences.

Colonial history

The history of Timor is primarily a record of colonial contact. The biggest attraction in Timor for colonialists was sandalwood, which for centuries had brought traders to the island. Early Chinese references to Timor which began during the Yüan dynasty of the twelfth and thirteenth centuries described Timor as a distant source of sandalwood. The trade may have been several centuries older than these first references, possibly as early as the seventh century AD. The Chinese used the sandalwood for incense and perfume, fans, boxes and coffins.

Attracted by beeswax and sandalwood, Javanese traders had also visited the island well before the first Europeans arrived in the sixteenth century; the panegyric *Nagara Kertagama* mentions Timor as being part of the realm of the Javanese kingdom of Majapahit.

Today, the chief product of sandalwood is the extraction of its oil, used for fixing perfumes, which is exported to France and the United States, while the waste powder is sold to Hong Kong, Taiwan and Singapore for use in incense.

The arrival of the Portuguese

In 1511 the port of Malacca fell (now Melaka in Malaysia) to Afonso de Albuquerque and in 1514 a fleet under the leadership of António de Abreu departed for the Moluccas, whose spices had attracted the attention of the world. They hoped to arrive at the island of Banda, famed for its nutmeg, by following the north coast of Java and the Lesser Sunda Islands.

With them were missionaries who met the spiritual needs of the sailors and introduced their faith to all of the places they called at. At first the Portuguese were not allowed by local rulers to set up any permanent posts on Timor so, in 1566, Dominican friars settled on Solor, an island to the north of Timor, where they built a fort to keep out Muslim attackers. They procured sandalwood by setting up entreposts (a small one had been set up in Lifau in the north west region of Oecussi in 1562) and entering into agreements with local rulers as well as dealing through their Topass middlemen.

Topasses

Around the fort in Solor grew up a settlement populated by offspring of Portuguese soldiers, sailors and traders from Malacca and Macau, who intermarried with local women. This mixed race of Christian faith, some of whom had arrived from Malacca when the city had been taken by the Dutch in 1641 and the majority of the city's Indo-Portuguese citizens had fled to Macassar and Larantuka, and the Christian natives connected with them, became known as Topasses (supposedly from the Dravidian for 'interpreter' *tupassi*).

Their descendants increased to around 12,000 by 1600, attaining an important place in the socio-political history of Flores and Timor as intermediaries in trade negotiations between the Portuguese (and the Dutch) and the native rulers, and as middlemen in the sandalwood trade. Much of their political power was attained by skilfully playing the Dutch and Portuguese off against each other. Timor became a patchwork of independent territories during the colonial period with changing claims of allegiances to either the Dutch or the Portuguese. Through the end of the colonial period a remarkable amount of local autonomy was preserved.

The Dutch took the Solor fort by force in 1613, displacing the Portuguese to Larantuka on the eastern tip of Flores, where the Topasses became known as Larantuquieros. The Larantuquieros received a fresh injection of European blood in 1629 when the Dutch commander from Solor, Jan de Hornay deserted to Larantuka, became a Roman Catholic and married a Timorese slave girl, having two sons. The de Hornay, or Ornay, family became one of the most powerful Topass families. Larantuka remained the Portuguese base for the rest of the seventeenth century.

Following persistent proselytizing the number of Catholics rose rapidly in Timor and a Portuguese fort was built on the site of present-day Kupang in 1640.

The arrival of the Dutch

The Dutch had previously concentrated their energies on the control of the Moluccan spice trade but, wanting a slice of the sandalwood trade, seized the fort at Kupang in 1653, changing its name to Fort Concordia. In retaliation the Portuguese summoned the powerful Topass families, the De Hornays and Da Costas from Larantuka and Solor, to help fight the Dutch.

In 1656 a Dutch expeditionary force under commander Arnold de Valming was thoroughly beaten in Amarasi by these Topass forces, scotching any Dutch expansion plans, isolating them in Fort Concordia, and reducing them to petty scheming, for nearly another century. Taking advantage of the breakdown of the Wewuki-Wehali confederacy following the punitive expedition by the Portuguese in 1642, the Dutch created a network of alliances and trade contacts with various native rulers on the western tip of Timor and on Roti, setting the pattern of population in Nusa Tenggara to this day.

Their success against the Dutch guaranteed a permanent Topass presence on Timor from that date. They settled in Lifau in Oecussi and began to exert increasing influence in sandalwood growing areas in the centre of the island. The Topasses grew increasingly powerful. Through local alliance and marriages, and brute force, they maintained their monopoly on the sandalwood trade.

In 1701 Portugal, preferring direct rule rather than ruling indirectly through the church and their unreliable Topass allies, claimed Timor as a colony, ruled out of Goa. They appointed a civil governor, António Coelho Guerreiro, and managed to install him in Lifau, marking the beginning of over 250 years of actual colonial Portuguese presence on the island.

As a result of local political wranglings the Topasses attacked Fort Concordia in November 1749. The Dutch defeated them at the Battle of Penfui, the site of modern Kupang's airport, allowing the Dutch to take control over a larger part of West Timor.

Twenty years later the Portuguese had to move from Lifau to Dili after their capital was seized by the Dutch, with the help of a Topass blockade on the settlement. The Portuguese and Dutch continued to manœuvre for power in the island, by manipulating the local chiefs, for nearly another hundred years until the island was divided by the two sides under the Treaty of Lisbon – drawn up in 1859, but not actually signed until just before the First World War.

In the late eighteenth century the Dutch controlled southwestern Timor, the Portuguese controlled the northeastern part and the Topasses controlled the central, sandalwood-rich portion. The Dutch invited the Portuguese to discuss the problem of frontiers, with meetings lasting for five years, from 1854 to 1859. With a compensation of 80,000 florins the islands of Flores and Solor and the once Topass-held lands in the centre of Timor were acceded to the Dutch and the Portuguese took control of Oecussi and the eastern part of Timor including the islands of Atauro and Jaco. The agreement was promulgated in 1913, fixing the political division of the island until the Indonesian annexation of East Timor and Oecussi in 1976.

The outbreak of the First World War came only only four years after the fall of the Portuguese monarchy and the establishment of the Republic. Timor was generally at a great distance from any of the theatres of war although Germany declared war on Portugal after it acted against the Germans in southwest and east Africa and requisitioned German vessels sheltering in her ports.

Throughout the whole of this colonial period, even in the days of Javanese trade contacts, the nature of Timorese society made it very difficult for any potential colonist to gain any meaningful control over the island. Traditional Timorese domains were characterized by a ritually powerful centre, maintained by prestige, from which emanated power defining the boundaries of the domain. As prestige waxed and waned the various domains became relatively more or less powerful. This, of course, proved problematic for colonial administrators who wanted to define the geographical boundaries of individual domains.

The dual leadership of such domains was also to prove most complicated. Besides the spiritual or ritual leader there was also an executive who carried out the practice of ruling. In terms of complementary duality the spiritual leader was 'female', being religious and conjunctive and the executive was 'male', dealing with the physical world.

Colonial administrators often neglected the need to work with both parties, without which their projects were doomed to failure. These manifestations of Timorese society are gradually lessening but proved effective in maintaining the identity of Timorese society during the colonial presence.

As the colonists found it impossible to rule absolutely, they sought instead to ensure that political control was dispersed enough that they could continue to trade. This resulted in many small kingdoms with little or no contact with colonizing forces, leading to the maintenance of much of Timorese identity well into the twentieth century.

The Rise of Indonesian nationalism

During the 1920s and 1930s young Indonesian nationalists, especially in Java, were forming political parties and associations, with the aim of securing independence in the future.

In 1933, several young Protestant Christians from Roti and Savu who were studying at the Bandung Institute of Technology in West Java formed an association called De Timorsch Jongeren, 'Timorese Youth'.

This was just one of a number of similar organizations being formed throughout the archipelago at that time, usually grouping together students from a particular part of the archipelago. They were intended to bind together these young people in a cultural and nationalistic association, helping to implant political aspirations through which they could work for eventual independence.

De Timorsch Jongeren was intended to unite all students from the Timor Residency who were studying in different regions of the Netherlands East Indies. The founder of this group was a Rotinese, H. Johannes (later joined by two others from the same island), and two Savunese, Sk. Tibuludji and I.H. Doko.

Doko returned to Kupang in 1937 after completing his studies, and turned De Timorsch Jongeren into a political association, Perserikatan Kebangsaan Timor, the 'Timor Nationalist Union', aimed at promoting and pursuing the goal of an independent Indonesia. The arrival of the Japanese in the island in 1942 gave political associations like this the chance to act for real change.

Second World War

War broke out in Europe in September 1939 with the Netherlands falling in 1940, but the East Indies remained in Free Dutch hands. Portugal remained neutral throughout the war.

Portugal, Britain, Australia and the Free Dutch consulted on defensive moves to assist Portuguese Timor in case of a possible attack by Japan, but Dutch and Australian forces landed near Dili on 17 December 1941, while there was still some doubt about Portuguese agreement in such a move. Its aim was to protect the colony against Japanese occupation.

Portuguese forces were despatched to take over from the Dutch and Australian forces, but failure by the Japanese to guarantee safe passage for the Portuguese troop-transport delayed the vessel en route. On 20 February 1942 Japanese forces entered Kupang. The Governor-General of the Netherlands East Indies, van Starkenborgh, resigned on 5 March 1942, leaving the military operations to the Commander-in-Chief of the Indies Armed Forces, General H. ter Poorten, who, realizing that the Japanese forces outnumbered his own inferior force, surrendered three days later, without informing the allied command.

When the Japanese entered Kupang, they met fierce resistance from Australian units but after suffering heavy casualties in fighting around the airfield at Penfui to the southeast of the town, the remnant of this Australian force were forced to make their escape into Portuguese Timor.

By 12 March the Japanese forces began thrusting out from Kupang towards the border between the two Timors. Before the Dutch administration had left they had formed a *stadswacht* and a *vernielingsdienst*, a group composed of Timorese and Savunese who were supposed to blow up installations and conduct a kind of 'scorched earth' policy.

Under the Japanese, I.H. Doko, the founder of the Perserikatan Kebangsaan Timor, became head of the Bunko – the Department of Health, Education and Information, as well as being the editor of the small paper Timor Syuho, in which he continued to publish (in Indonesian) nationalist ideas. Like many Indonesians, he saw the Japanese as the means by which the myth of Dutch supremacy had been broken; this gave him a promise of future independence.

Upon the arrival of Japanese troops in Portuguese Timor the 400 members of the 2/2 and 2/4 Australian Independent Companies withdrew to the mountains from where they organized a guerilla war against the Japanese, holding down a force of some 20,000 Japanese before evacuation to Darwin. They managed to kill 1,500 of the enemy for a loss of 40, before being evacuated from the south coast in early 1943.

The success of, what became known as, the Sparrow Force was in diverting a measure of Japanese attention at a critical time, and perhaps, in part led to a build up of Japanese forces on Timor during 1942 in anticipation of possible Allied attempts to reoccupy the island. The Japanese officially respected Portuguese sovereignty, and in doing so hoped to safeguard Portugal's neutral stance in the face of a second Allied invasion.

A number of Portuguese were evacuated along with the Australians. There were sharp divisions within the Portuguese community in Timor in respect of collaboration with the Allied forces, both before and after the Japanese landings. Many of those Portuguese who remained in Timor for the duration of the occupation lost their lives or underwent great privations. The majority of the remaining Portuguese were forced into a zone of concentration at Liquiça to await the outcome of the war.

The Timorese suffered greatly from starvation and retribution from the occupying Japanese forces: it is thought that some 70,000 died during the war.

East Timor was restored to Portuguese adminstrative control at a transfer ceremony at Dili on 26 September 1945 following the acceptance of Japanese surrender in Timor at Kupang on 11 September 1945.

Indonesian independence

On 17 August 1945 the Netherlands East Indies had declared its independence from the Netherlands, becoming Indonesia. This started a long round of discussion and military conflict resulting in complete independence in 1950.

Adminstratively, under the Netherlands East Indies government, West Timor had been included in the Province of the Celebes, (later called the province of the Greater East) with Macassar (Ujung Pandang) as the capital. There was a Resident in Kupang, who had responsibility for all of the Lesser Sundas Islands except Bali, with an Assistant Resident in Ende, Flores.

The Malino conference in July 1946 introduced a plan for a federal form of government in Kalimantan and Nusa Tenggara with some form of continuing Dutch connection. A State of East Indonesia was created in Denpasar, Bali, in December 1946. This was called Negara Indonesia Timur and was ultimately part of a greater United States of Indonesia.

Despite continuing Dutch control, nationalist ideas were strong. I.H. Doko was cabinet minister in the successive cabinets of Anak Agung Gde Agung, Prime Minister of the State of Eastern Indonesia. In Timor in 1945 Doko had brought the Perserikatan Kebangsaan Timor back to life in the form of the Partai Demokrasi Indonesia the 'Indonesian Democracy Party'. Together with H.A. Koroh, the raja of Amarasi and chairman of the Dewan Raja-raja Timor, 'Council of Timorese Rajas' he established branches of the party in Roti, Savu, Sumbawa and Flores.

In 1950 the State of Eastern Indonesia was absorbed into the unitary Republic of Indonesia along with the other federal states which had made up the United States of Indonesia.

Since 1958 the Indonesian government has placed Timor and Roti in the province of Nusa Tenggara Timur, with its capital in Kupang. This province, comprising all of the Lesser Sunda islands except Bali, Lombok and Sumbawa, reflects the cultural and religious affiliations of the majority of the population.

The church and revival

The church has been active in Timor since the first Western contacts and most Timorese would today profess to some sort of Christianity, although in many cases this is only a thin veneer over a deeper vein of traditional animist religion.

In West Timor the church became autonomous in 1947 under the name of the Gereja Masehi Injili Timor (GMIT), the 'Evangelical Christian Church of Timor'.

Introduction

A Revival or 'Spiritual movement' occurred in some strength during the middle and late 1960s. It was a fundamentalist movement which affected thousands of Protestants in Timor and Roti, including many of those who had converted to Christianity during the military campaign following an attempted 'coup' in 1965. The zeal and inspiration engendered by this movement, while appealing to Timorese Protestants, passed the Catholics by.

The movement emphasized and found its point in the miracles of healing, and raising the dead, which its leaders claimed they could perform. Throughout 1964 and 1965 there were increasing numbers of reports of miracle cures and the laying on of hands from throughout West Timor.

Not the first movement of the Holy Spirit, revivals had also occurred in 1921 in Kisol, in 1926 on the south east coast and in 1942 and 1954 in Central Timor. They are seen by some as manifestations of stress and thus the revival of the mid–1960s could be attributable to the political and economic uncertainties preceding and following the 'coup' of September 1965.

The events of 1965

During the night of 30 September/1 October 1965 a small band of junior army officers organized the kidnapping and killing of six generals of the Indonesian Army High Command in a coup designed to prevent this pro-Western Council of Generals in their apparent intention to take charge of the country, in order to make sure that President Sukarno's policies could continue free from the intrigues of the generals.

General Suharto, head of the army's Strategic Command, quickly had the situation in hand and dispersed the rebels. The army has always taken the line that it rescued the President from the machinations of the Partai Komunis Indonesia, the 'Indonesian Communist Party'. It is still not known whether these rebels were Communists or not.

Once the attempted coup had been put down in Jakarta, there began a full-scale military operation throughout the whole of the country with the avowed aim to eradicate all members of the Indonesian Communist Party and those who supported and sympathized with them. Reports began to reach the outside world that the rounding up of dissidents had degenerated into wholesale blood-letting and that there were no trials of communists; the army or those deputed by them were simply killing communists and their sympathizers – or even those suspected of being sympathetic to the Indonesian Communist Party – out of hand.

In Timor, the state university, Universitas Nusa Cendana, in Kupang, had been founded in 1962 and some of its intellectuals and teachers were members of the Communist Party. In Kupang, Soe, and in other towns of Central and West Timor, there was a certain amount of Communist infiltration into the Protestant churches.

As in other parts of Indonesia, especially Java and Bali where there were many landless peasants and where the Communist Party based their local manifesto on land reform, so in Timor some of the Protestant priests became Communists because of the concern for the poverty of their people. They saw it as a party that cared for the impoverished often in a more Christian way than some of the churches.

Undoubtedly many of the Timorese who were caught were in fact communists virtually by accident. Often the local teacher or priest told them to put their mark on a card: having done so, they were then told that they were members of the Communist Party. The villagers often had little knowledge of the political implications of their actions, nor any understanding of communist ideology. Many saw it as a progressive party and an organization that appeared to be concerned for their welfare.

Killings in the north and Catholic area of Timor seem to have been substantially lower than in the south and central parts though figures are lacking. Most of the Christians who were members of the Communist Party appear to have been Protestants.

Timor's recent history

Since the mid–1970s the story of Timor has been that of the Indonesian annexation of East Timor in 1975 and its aftermath. There are a number of relatively cheap and easily available paperbacks discussing the subject so it is intended to give here only the bare bones of the events and allow the reader to fill out the details with individual reading.

Portugal's new administration in April 1974, following the overthrow of the Caetano Government, was committed to allowing the colonies, including East Timor, to exercise their right to self-determination.

It became legal to form political parties and two main parties emerged: the Frente Revolucionária de Timor Leste Independente (Fretilin) and the União Democrática Timorense (UDT). Both parties were committed to East Timor's eventual independence. Fretilin wanted this promptly, while the UDT proposed a gradual process involving an extended association with Portugal, possibly within the framework of a commonwealth of Portuguese-speaking countries.

Of several smaller parties formed after April 1974, the Associação

Popular Democrática Timorense (Apodeti), favoured integration with Indonesia, and on that basis took on an enhanced significance in the affairs of the territory before and after the invasion.

Portugal was open to any solution, including integration with Indonesia, as long as it was the result of the free choice of the Timorese population, in accordance with international law and United Nations resolutions.

In January 1975, a local programme of decolonization was started, mainly through the restructuring of local government and the reorganization of the educational system. Teaching methods and curricula, previously identical to those of metropolitan Portugal, were tailored for Timor. Administrative reform led, in August 1975, to popular elections for the regional administration of Lautem district.

A coalition forged between Fretilin and UDT in January 1975, working towards independence within five to ten years, broke down in May of the same year, and by August relations between the two parties had deteriorated to the extent that, on the night of 10 August, UDT instigated a coup against the Portuguese authorities in Dili, in a bid to pre-empt a Fretilin-led push for independence.

In the ensuing fighting between forces allied to Fretilin and the UDT, the Portuguese governor, Lemos Pires, withdrew himself and his staff to the island of Atauro. By 27 August, Dili was completely under Fretilin's control.

By late September UDT had withdrawn into the Indonesian part of the island and announced that they now favoured integration with Indonesia. Fretilin conducted what was, by many accounts, an effective administration while awaiting the return of the Portuguese authorities to complete the decolonization process. When the Portuguese authorities did not return, and following an escalation of fighting along the Indonesian border, Fretilin proclaimed an independent Democratic Republic of East Timor on 28 November 1975 and appealed for international recognition and support. The pro-Indonesian parties responded with a declaration of integration with Indonesia.

On 7 December, Indonesian forces landed troops by sea and air in Dili and Baucau, with Indonesia claiming that these towns were being liberated by UDT and Apodeti with the help of Indonesian volunteers. On 18 December 1975 the formation of a Provisional Government of East Timor was announced, with the presidents of Apodeti and the UDT as respectively chief and deputy chief executives.

Fretilin withdrew to the interior to fight an armed struggle against Indonesian troops. Their numbers and their impact have been limited, but their struggle continues, and in an effort to pacify them the Indonesian army has undertaken a number of military campaigns, most notoriously Operasi Keamanan (Operation Security), from April to September 1981, in which thousands of civilians are reported to have been deployed in human 'fences' to converge on remaining Fretilin positions.

On 31 May 1976 it was announced that a People's Representative Assembly had met in Dili and had approved a petition calling for integration with Indonesia. On 17 July 1976 President Suharto signed the Bill of Integration, passed by the Indonesian parliament, into law, and East Timor was proclaimed as Indonesia's twenty-seventh province, Timor Timur.

In the years following the invasion the United Nations General Assembly each year passed a motion reaffirming East Timor's right to self-determination and calling for negotiations between Fretilin and the Indonesian and Portuguese governments. The industrialized nations, and many African, Asian and Latin American states voted with Indonesia against the motion. Many smaller states tended to support East Timorese independence, as did other former Portuguese colonies.

Since 1982 the motion has not been resubmitted for debate because the United Nations Secretary General was charged with exploring avenues for achieving a comprehensive settlement of the problem.

It is estimated that about 200,000 people have died in East Timor since Indonesian invasion directly as a result of the armed conflict, about a third of the pre-invasion population. Those who have died include those killed during bombardments, armed encounters, and as a result of famine and disease, as well as those reported to have been executed upon surrender or capture. Following a visit to Indonesia in November 1991, a United Nations Special Rapporteur on Torture concluded that in politically unstable regions, torture is routine. It is likely that East Timor falls within the category of politically unstable.

East Timor once again became world news in November 1991 when Indonesian troops fired on mourners after a memorial mass at the Santa Cruz cemetery, Dili, killing up to 200 people. The incident followed a period of mounting tension following the cancellation of a planned visit by Portuguese parliamentarians to East Timor.

Portugal has declared its willingness to cooperate fully with the United Nations, in accordance with United Nations declarations on the concession of independence to colonial peoples and territories. In doing so, Portugal has recognized the status of East Timor as a non-autonomous territory, and acknowledged its own rôle as administering power. This is the legal framework which the United Nations and other international organizations have repeatedly recognized and affirmed.

Introduction

This situation has been made more complex by the other major development in Timor in recent years: the Timor Gap Zone of Cooperation Treaty. Signed by Indonesia and Australia on 11 December 1989, it is intended to pave the way for the exploitation of large oil reserves, thought to be one of the twenty richest oil deposits in the world (five million barrels oil and 50,000 billion cubic feet of natural gas; *Far Eastern Economic Review* 19 April 1984), that lie in the sea bed within the former border zone of Portuguese Timor and Australia.

Portugal has presented a complaint at the International Court of Human Rights against the Treaty, stating that it violates international law, is lacking in respect for the resolutions approved by the United Nations General Assembly and Security Council, and totally disregards the legitimate interests of the people of East Timor; that is, of a non-autonomous territory under Portuguese administration.

West Timor, blessed with the political stability its neighbour lacks, since 1950 has been undergoing a slow but steady process of economic development, a process which looks to become rather more rapid with the present stress on developing Eastern Indonesia, of which Nusa Tenggara Timur is a part.

Nusa Tenggara Timur has a remote and disadvantaged regional economy, traditionally because of climatic limitations, but also because of the adverse effects on Nusa Tenggara Timur of Indonesia-wide trade policies which favour areas of concentrated industry and international ports such as Java, while penalizing agricultural commodity-producing regions including Nusa Tenggara Timur. Other disadvantages include the already-degraded environment, poor infrastructures, physical remoteness, lack of entrepreneurship and training. The cultural richness and elaborate social structures of the region are also seen by some as hindrances to development.

Concluding remarks

Development priorities in West Timor include, firstly, meeting the subsistence needs of the people allowing developmental innovations and ideas to be introduced without compromising food-availability or income levels and, secondly, providing physical and social infrastructures.

Agriculture, with its major subsistence and employment rôle, must receive prime attention, especially the main subsistence crops of maize and dryland rice, and secondly the cash crops of coffee and cocoa, as well as cattle, presently the most dynamic sector of the economy. Fishing will probably also be a good economic investment, as well as tourism, where there are excellent opportunities for local peoples in providing services. There are important opportunites in downstream processing, in the fishing and coffee sectors, for example. Finally, but not the least of the possibilites, is the development of the broad-based village weaving industry with its unique product.

The future of East Timor is, sadly, rather more complex. The Indonesian administration can be credited with developing the territory in a physical sense to a higher level than under Portuguese administration. But these developments are to be viewed in the light of reduced personal freedoms and the lack of progress in translating these developments into benefits for the Timorese people themselves.

The achievement of an agreed settlement on the future of East Timor, whether total independence or continued association with Indonesia, depends largely on the willingness of governments, corporations and international organizations to become actively involved in the process. Many nations in the Western and non-aligned blocs, it can be argued, have ignored East Timor in favour of lucrative concessions and strategic advantages in Indonesia, or ideological considerations. Many would suggest that there needs to be a review of the policy of implicitly accepting Indonesia's incorporation of East Timor which, it is clear, has not been willingly accepted by the East Timorese.

References

East of Bali: from Lombok to Timor. Text and photographs by Kal Muller, edited by David Pickell. Berkeley, California: Singapore: Periplus, 1991.

East Timor: violations of human rights: extrajudicial executionns, 'disappearances', torture and political imprisonment, 1975–1984. London: Amnesty International Publications, 1985.

Harvest of the palm: ecological change in eastern Indonesia. James. J. Fox. Cambridge, Massachusetts: Harvard University Press, 1977.

Indonesia's forgotten war: the hidden history of East Timor. John G. Taylor. London: Zed, 1991.

Nusa Tenggara Timur: the challenges of development. Edited by Colin Barlow, Alex Bellis, Kate Andrews. Canberra: Australian National University, Department of Political and Social Change, Research School of Pacific Studies, 1991. 294p. (Political and Social Change Monograph, no. 12).

Palms and the cross: socio-economic development in Nusatenggara, 1930–1975. Rex Alexander Francis Paul Webb. Townsville, Australia: James Cook University of North Queensland, 1986. (Centre for Southeast Asian Studies Monograph, no. 15).

The sickle and the cross: christians and communists in Bali, Flores,

Introduction

Sumba and Timor, 1965–67. Rex Alexander Francis Paul Webb. *Journal of Southeast Asian Studies*, vol. 17, no. 1 (March 1986), p. 94–112.

Names and Orthography

Names and the standardization of terms are difficulties faced in conducting any research on Timor. In West Timor and Roti, over the past forty years, the names tend to have attained at least a standardized Indonesian form. East Timor is in the process of changing from Portuguese to Indonesian spellings so I have used the Portuguese versions for the sake of continuity and in recognition of the, as yet, undecided political status of the territory. Two names which have actually changed under Indonesian usage are Oecussi which has become the Indonesian *kabupaten* of Ambenu, and the little island of Atauro is known as Pulau Kambing.

The names of Timor's ethnolinguistic groups appear in differing forms depending on the language used by the particular author. They have been standardized as follows: Bunak (for Buna, Buna', Bunaq), Cairui (Kairui), Ema (Kemak), Mambai (Mambae), Makassai (Makassae), Tetun (Teto, Tetum, Belu), Waimaka (Uia Ma'a). Roti and Ndao are sometimes seen as Rote and Ndau. In much Dutch anthropological work the term 'Timorese' refers to Atoni. Titles of references have been quoted verbatim regardless of spellings, but annotations use the standardized spellings.

Portuguese personal names consist, in their most basic form, of a given name, the father's family name and the mother's family name. They have been listed according to the final element, except when an author has consistently published under one of the other elements. For example, Ruy Cinatti Vaz Monteiro Gomes (Ruy Cinatti). Chinese names have been listed according to the first element.

Chronology

12th century	First Chinese mention, during the Yüan dynasty, of sandalwood trading in Timor
1514	António de Abreu makes the first Western sighting of Timor
1566	The Portuguese establish a fort in Solor, from where they conduct sandalwood trading expeditions to Timor
1642	The power of the Wewuki-Wehali confederacy of Timorese kingdoms is broken by the Portuguese
1653	The Dutch seize Fort Concordia, founded at Kupang by the Portuguese in 1640
1656	Dutch beaten by Topasses in Amarasi, guaranteeing permanent Topass presence in Timor; and restricting Dutch influence in the island
1701	Portuguese civil administration of Timor begins under António Coelho Guerreiro at Lifau
1749	Battle of Penfui; the Dutch, beating the Topasses, become more influential in western Timor
1769	Portuguese administration moved from Lifau to Dili

1859	Treaty of Lisbon determining the border between the Dutch and Portuguese halves of the island. Not ratified until 1913
1933	Formation of De Timorsch Jongeren, a nationalist X-organization seeking independence for Indonesia. In 1937 it became Perserikatan Kebangsaan Timor
1942–1945	Japanese occupation
17 August 1945	Indonesia declares independence from the Netherlands
1946	Negara Indonesia Timur created within the United States of Indonesia
1950	West Timor becomes part of the newly-formed unitary Republic of Indonesia
1958	Administratively, West Timor becomes part of the province of Nusa Tenggara Timur
30 September 1965	'Communist coup' in Indonesia
25 April 1974	Armed Forces Movement overthrow Caetano régime in Portugal which opens the way for the decolonization of East Timor
10 August 1975	Civil war breaks out between UDT and Fretilin
26 August 1975	Portuguese governor abandons Dili as civil war rages
28 November 1975	Fretilin declares independence and proclaims the Democratic Republic of East Timor
7 December 1975	Indonesian troops enter Dili
17 July 1976	President Suharto signs Bill of Integration, annexing East Timor as the twenty-seventh province of Indonesia, Timor Timur

11 December 1989 Indonesia and Australia sign the Timor Gap Treaty paving the way for the exploitation of offshore oil reserves between East Timor and Australia.

The Island and its People

1 **Indonesia: a country study.**
Edited by Frederica M. Bunge. Washington, DC: Army Department
HQ, 1983. 4th ed. 343p. map. bibliog. (American University Foreign
Area Studies).
This volume provides a concise introduction to Indonesia and allows Timor to be
placed within its present context. The main subdivisions are: history (Donald M.
Seekins); society and environment (Riga Adiwoso-Suprapto); economy (Stephen B.
Wickman); government and politics (Rinn-Sup Shinn); and national security (Melinda
W. Cooke).

2 **Timor Português.** (Portuguese Timor.)
Hélio Augusto Esteves Felgas. Lisbon: Agência Geral do Ultramar,
1956. 570p. map. bibliog.
Despite its age, this book contains much that is still relevant and it remains an
important introduction to colonial East Timor. The subjects covered include physical
geography, flora and fauna, ethnolinguistic groups, a history of Portuguese administration and development efforts.

3 **Dutch Timor and the Lesser Sunda islands.**
Foreign Office. London: HMSO, 1919. 38p. (Handbooks prepared
under the direction of the Historical Section of the Foreign Office, no.
75).
This pamphlet, as with the one on *Portuguese Timor* (q.v.), was prepared to provide
British diplomats with information in a convenient form – geography, economy,
history, society, religion and politics – concerning the districts with which they might
have to deal. It is now largely out-of-date, but provides a fair snapshot on the state of
the region during the early part of the century.

1

4 **Portuguese Timor.**
   Foreign Office.   London: HMSO, 1920. 26p. (Handbooks prepared
   under the direction of the Historical Section of the Foreign Office, no.
   80.)

Used in conjunction with item number three this provides a fair description of the
physical state of the island at the time of writing.

5 **Aspectos de Timor.** (Views of Timor.)
   Photographs by Ruy Cinatti Vaz Monteiro Gomes.   *Garcia de Orta*, vol.
   1, no. 1 (1953).

Timor's dramatic landscape, vibrantly-coloured costume and religious and social
tradition have provided plenty of material for photographers during the past decades.
These early photographs by Ruy Cinatti and Helder Lains e Silva (q.v.) remain some
of the most powerfully atmospheric visual impressions of the island.

6 **Gentes e terras de Timor.** (Timorese people and landscapes.)
   Photographs by Helder Lains e Silva.   *Garcia de Orta*, vol. 3, no. 4
   (1955).

No less stunning, this set of photographs is more documentary, with short captions and
more coverage of the Timorese people.

East of Bali: from Lombok to Timor.
See item no. 9.

Asia Yearbook.
See item no. 335.

Indonesia: an official handbook.
See item no. 338.

Travel Guides

7 **Indonesia: a travel survival kit.**
   Joe Cummings, Susan Forsyth, John Noble, Alan Samagalski, Tony
   Wheeler.   Hawthorn, Australia; Berkeley, California: Lonely Planet,
   1990. 2nd ed. 896p. map.

Regular flights to Kupang from Darwin in Australia, and the opening up of East Timor
to tourists in January 1989, have put Timor firmly on the tourist trail. Tourist guides of
this sort prove invaluable on any journey through Indonesia; up-to-date, clear
information saves time and keeps disappointment to a minimum. There is advice on
accommodation, tourist sights, transport and food, street maps of Kupang and Dili as
well as a section on the island of Roti, reached from Kupang. Covering the whole of
the archipelago, this is a fairly large and heavy book, but invaluable for anyone visiting
Timor as part of a longer journey through the islands. Lonely Planet also publish the
handy pocket-sized *Indonesia phrasebook* by Margit Meinhold (South Yarra,
Australia, 1984. 64p.).

8 **Indonesia handbook.**
   Bill Dalton.   Chico, California: Moon Publications, 1991. 5th ed. 1,072p.
   map.

The fifth edition of this book, after nearly twenty years of guiding travellers through
Indonesia, indicates the success and popularity of its style. The breadth of its coverage
and information is similar to the *Travel survival kit* (q.v.), but the entries are longer
and more anecdotal, and the book as a whole is larger.

9 **East of Bali: from Lombok to Timor.**
   Text and photographs by Kal Muller, edited by David Pickell.   Berkeley,
   California; Singapore: Periplus, 1991. 285p. map. bibliog.

This is the ideal choice for those who are only visiting the islands of Nusa Tenggara. It
is well-produced, lavishly illustrated with photographs and has excellent, informed
essays by eminent authorities on the region: geography (David Wall); prehistory (Peter

Travel Guides

Bellwood), history and people (James J. Fox) and religion (Coen Pepplinkhuizen). Roti is covered in detail, and James J. Fox introduces the small island of Ndao, and describes the history of Kupang during colonial times.

Travellers' Accounts

Early

10   A descriptive dictionary of the Indian Islands and adjacent countries.
John Crawfurd.   Singapore: Oxford University Press, 1971. 459p. map.
The author served in the British administration of Java under Sir Thomas Raffles from 1811–1816. This facsimile edition of the original published in 1856 shows the author to be consistently objective in the presentation of statistical and descriptive information; he includes an entry on the camel in order to explain that the animal is unknown in southeast Asia.

11   A voyage to New Holland.
William Dampier.   London: Argonaut, 1939. 266p. maps.
This is the first British account of Timor, and is one of the most detailed descriptions of the island for the seventeenth century. Dampier arrived in Timor in September 1699 to take on water and make repairs to his ship, the *Roebuck*, and spent three months there. He called at Kupang and Lifau in Oecussi, but never reached Dili. This is edited with introductory notes and illustrative documents by James A. Williamson.

12   Unbeaten tracks in the islands of the Far East: experiences of a naturalist's wife in the 1880's.
Anna Forbes.   Singapore: Oxford University Press, 1987. 305p. map.
In the preface to the original edition of this book (published as *Insulinde*: *experiences of a naturalist's wife* in 1887), the author suggests that those not attracted to her husband's work (*H.O. Forbes: a naturalist's wanderings in the Eastern archipelago* [q.v.]) 'because of the admixture of scientific matter, may find some interest in reading my simpler account'. Mrs Forbes' account may be less scientific, but is no less a testament to the commitment and strength of the Victorian traveller, particularly the final part with the fever-stricken author awaiting her husband's return from plant-hunting in the interior.

13 **A naturalist's wanderings in the eastern archipelago.**
Henry O. Forbes.   Singapore: Oxford University Press, 1989. 536p.
map.

Forbes travelled through the archipelago, mainly following in the footsteps of Alfred
Russel Wallace, but his journey through the interior of Timor is a journey that Wallace
never made. As with Wallace, Forbes made valuable collections and descriptions of
birds, butterflies and beetles, but his interest in local ethnic groups also shows and his
vivid descriptions of his journey make captivating reading. There is an introduction by
the Earl of Cranbrook.

14 **Infortunes d'un prince de Timor accueilli en France sous Louis XV.** (The
misfortunes of a Timorese prince in France during the reign of Louis
XV.)
Anne Lombard-Jourdan.   *Archipel*, no. 16 (1978), p. 91–133. map.

A reverse travel account describing a Timorese person's travels to the West. Pascal
Jean Balthazard Celse, Prince of Timor and Solor, was born in Animata, south of
Lifau, the son of Gaspar da Costa, a powerful Topass (i.e. of mixed European and
native descent) ally of the Portuguese in Oecussi. His tutor, Père Ignace, a Portuguese
Dominican friar took him to Macau in 1743 to continue his education and in 1750 they
arrived in the French port of Lorient. Père Ignace abandoned the prince on the quay
and he died in obscurity in France, never returning to Timor, after searching in vain
for his tutor.

15 **Une mémoire inédit de F.E. de Rosily sur l'île de Timor (1772).** (The
unedited memoirs of F.E. de Rosily from the island of Timor [1772].)
Anne Lombard-Jourdan.   *Archipel*, no. 23 (1982), p. 75–104. map.

François-Etienne de Rosily (1748–1832), a young naval officer, visited Timor's
northeast coast from 8 May to 15 June 1772, a break in his journey aboard a French
ship of war from Port Louis (Mauritius) via the Kerguelen Islands and Australia's west
coast to Timor, and back to Port Louis via the roads of Batavia. The author gives some
biographical information about de Rosily and further details of the entire journey. The
report itself concludes with various concise details concerning the geography, climate,
fauna, population, agriculture, mining, fishing, hunting, public health, law, arms and
warfare, government, religion and language.

16 **Journal of a rambler – the journal of John Boultbee.**
Edited by June Starke.   Auckland, New Zealand: Oxford University
Press, 1986. 225p. map. bibliog.

John Boultbee, an Englishman born near Nottingham, arrived in Tasmania in 1823 at
the age of twenty three and spent the next ten years whaling and sealing around the
Bass Straits and in New Zealand. In January 1833 he sailed for Timor aboard the
whaler *Sir Francis McNaghton* and spent until mid-April of that year whaling
unsuccessfully along the northern coast, trading in the ports. Besides the entertaining
writings of Boultbee himself, the editor has provided the reader with much background
information.

17 **The Malay archipelago: the land of the orang-utan and the bird of paradise. A narrative of travel with studies of man and nature.**
Alfred Russel Wallace. Singapore: Oxford University Press, 1986. 635p. map.
Wallace visited Kupang in 1857 and 1859, and Dili in 1861 during his travels through the archipelago. He devotes two chapters of this book to Timor. The first contains observations of the island, its people and their lifestyle, while the second describes the bird species of Timor and their relations to Javanese and Australian avifaunas. Introduction by John Bastin.

Chinese navigators in Insulinde about AD 1500.
See item no. 271.

20th century

18 **Indonesia and Portuguese Timor.**
John Cockcroft. Sydney: Angus & Robertson, 1969. 128p. map.
A good selection of photographs accompanies this enthusiastic description of some tourist sites: the Casa de Timor handicrafts centre which 'did not sell anything made with machines', and the Timor Oil base near Viqueque. It is unlikely whether either of the aforementioned attractions still exist, but the large limestone caves, sulphur springs and volcanoes of mud also described by the author give some idea of future tourism potential.

19 **Reanimated relic.**
Willard A. Hanna. *American Universities Field Staff Southeast Asia Series*, vol. 14, nos. 7, 8, 9 (April, May 1966). bibliog. Part 1: Target Timor, Part 2: Dili, Part 3: Religion, commerce and travel.
Armed with letters of introduction and journalistic experience the author was able to make the most of a week's stay in Portuguese Timor. The first part is a very good account of Portuguese Timorese history and economy based on published sources available at the time. He then gives his personal impressions of Dili and its colonial life: the governor, Portuguese and Chinese businessmen, the Indonesian consul and some Australian school teachers. He is unable to meet any of the indigenous Timorese population of Dili, but describes some aspects of life in the rest of the province during the latter part of his visit.

20 **Eden to paradise.**
Margaret King. London: Hodder & Stoughton, 1963. 186p.
The author, an Australian anthropologist, visited the island twice and this travelogue contains descriptions of the scenery, dance and other aspects of East Timorese life.

21 **Timor: an untroubled Portuguese colony.**
Richard P. Momsen. *Geographical Magazine* (London), vol. 41, no.9
(June 1969), p. 680–88. map.
A decent overview of the geography, and some good photographs, of Portuguese
Timor. An optimistic review of Portuguese development attempts reports that *per
capita* income at that time was higher than that of Thailand and more than twice that of
Indonesia.

22 **Zwerftocht door Timor en onderhoorigheden.** (A journey through Timor
and its dependencies.)
W.O.J. Niewenkamp. Amsterdam: Elsevier, 1925. 176p. map.
There is no need to be able to read Dutch to appreciate the beauty of this large-format
'coffee table' travel book. Essentially a diary of the author's travels through Timor and
neighbouring islands in 1918, it is illustrated with monochrome sketches and washes,
and the text is embellished in stylized Timorese motifs.

23 **Timor: long waits and mad dashes.**
Dorothy West Pelzer. In: *Trek across Indonesia.* By Dorothy West
Pelzer. Singapore: Graham Brash, 1982, p. 29–35.
The author, having studied at the Bauhaus school of design, travelled through
Indonesia between May and December 1965, making a photographic record of
traditional house forms. Although none of the photographs are reproduced here, the
author shows a trained eye for detail in her lively and entertaining descriptions of visits
to Kupang, Atapupu and Atambua.

24 **The drums of Tonkin: an adventure in Indonesia.**
Frank Schreider, Helen Schreider. London: Frederick Muller, 1965.
268p. map.
The Schreiders travelled to Portuguese Timor in their sea-going jeep, and travelled
through the province for two weeks as guests of the governor. Their journey along the
north coast towards Indonesia at the end of their stay highlights transport difficulties
imposed by the terrain and climate. Their story is also told in classic travelogue style in
'East from Bali: by seagoing jeep to Timor' in *The National Geographic Magazine*, vol.
122, no. 2 (Aug. 1962), p. 236–79. map. This, of course, contains a selection of colour
photographs, one of which is of a ceremony during which some of the participants
'dance a martial step hours after a pre-dawn headhunter jubilee'.

25 **Notas extraídas do meu diário no decurso de uma expedição a Timor,
quando ali se encontravam as tropas japoneses.** (Notes from my diary
during an expedition to Japanese-occupied Timor.)
José de Freitas Soares. *Boletim de Arquivo História Militar,* no. 49
(1979), p. 57–152.
The author arrived in Timor a few months after the Japanese surrender, following
several months in Mozambique. The diary is a day-to-day record of the events of his
trip and return to Portugal in April 1946.

26 **Timor: a key to the Indies.**
Stuart St. Clair. *The National Geographic Magazine*, vol. 84, no. 3
(Sept. 1943), p. 355–84. map.

This fairly lengthy account is the product of a geologist's visit to Timor just before the
Second World War. Some good photographs compensate for the rather poor text.

27 **A forgotten outpost.**
Michael Teague. *Geographical Magazine* (London), vol. 37, no. 2
(June 1964), p. 110–23. map.

A dated but pleasantly atmospheric account of life in Portuguese Timor. Many aspects
of the economy and administration are described in a sketchy manner and are
accompanied by some fair photographs. Rather taken with its sleepy backwater
ambience, the author concludes with unintended irony: 'it would be a pity if
Portuguese Timor became the setting for yet another trumped up colonial quarrel'.

Contemporary

28 **Mud, sweat and tears.**
Annabel Sutton. In: *The islands in between: travels in Indonesia*.
London: Impact, 1989. p. 178–203. map.

Chapter nine of this book recounts the visit of two female travellers to Kupang and
Savu, illustrating vividly the ups and downs of the budget traveller (and the not-so-
budget traveller) in Indonesia today. The author expresses very clearly some of the
feelings of despair and resignation likely to be felt by most travellers at some point in
their travels. This should be required reading for anyone setting off for those 'thirteen
thousand islands like emeralds scattered in an azure sea' of holiday brochure fame.

29 **'Opening up': travellers' impressions of East Timor, 1989–1991.**
Edited by Kirsty Sword, Pat Walsh. Melbourne: Australia East Timor
Association, 1991. 50p.

This collection of travellers' accounts covers the period between East Timor opening
its borders to tourists in January 1989 and April 1991. Being relatively free to speak to
whom they like and visit the places of their choice, tourists provide a unique insight
into East Timorese life today. Shirley Shackleton, whose husband was one of the five
journalists killed during an Indonesian military attack on Balibo in October 1975,
focuses on women. Paddy Kenneally returned to East Timor in April 1990 for the first
time since he was there as a member of the Australian 2/2 Independent Company
between December 1941 and December 1942. Some of the other reports are
anonymous.

Geography

30 **Harvest of the palm: ecological change in eastern Indonesia.**
James J. Fox. Cambridge, Massachusetts: Harvard University Press,
1977. 290p. maps. bibliog.

Despite their harsh climates, the two smallest islands of the outer arc of the Lesser
Sunda islands, Roti and Savu, have historically had higher population densities than
the two larger islands, Timor and Sumba. The author examines the economic base that
supports these high population densities and notes that the populations of the two
islands get a significant proportion of their dietary requirement from the juice of the
inflorescence of the lontar palm, *Borassus sundaicus*. This food source is unaffected by
the severe dry season, unlike the swidden (shifting cultivation) fields of traditional
Timorese and Sumbanese agriculture and the islanders therefore live without the threat
of crop failure. This book focuses first on the ecological and economic situation, as it
existed at the time of writing, on the four islands and then on the historical
circumstances and external pressures that have fostered present-day adaptations.

31 **Man and environment in eastern Indonesia: a geoecological analysis of the
Baucau–Viqueque area as a possible basis for regional planning.**
Joachim K. Metzner. Canberra: Australian National University, 1977.
380p. maps. bibliog. (Development Studies Centre Monograph, no. 8).

The study concludes that the population of the study area lived under harsh physical
conditions and in disequilibrium with the environment. In coming to this conclusion
the author describes the population, the administration and settlement, the physical
factors of the environment and types of land use and land ownership, followed by an
analysis of this environment in its ecological context. The author concludes that
planning is needed, and includes a chapter on aspects of regional planning in the study
area.

32 **The Timor problem: a geographical interpretation of an underdeveloped island.**
Ferdinand Jan Ormeling. Groningen, The Netherlands: O.B. Wolters; The Hague: Martinus Nijhoff, 1956. 248p. maps. bibliog. Reprinted in New York: AMS Press, 1989. 296p.

This work remains unchallenged as the standard work in its field. It has straightforward and informative chapters, based on fieldwork undertaken in West Timor by the former head of the Geographical Institute in Jakarta, on the physical environment, the human factor and how the two combine to create unique problems in any effort to develop Timor.

33 **Frontiers of Asia and Southeast Asia.**
J.R.V. Prescott, H.J. Collier, D.F. Prescott. Melbourne, Australia: Melbourne University Press, 1977. 91p. map.

Case study no. 40 in this book is the first detailed description of the state of the boundaries between West and East Timor, and their evolution through various Luso-Dutch treaties. There is a map on the facing page. No. 38 details Indonesia's maritime boundaries with Australia and Papua New Guinea, including the area known as the Timor Gap.

34 **O clima e o solo de Timor: suas relações com a agricultura.** (The climate and soil of Timor, their relations with agriculture.)
Firmino António Soares. Lisbon: Junta de Investigações do Ultramar, 1957. 118p. map. bibliog. (Estudos, Ensaios e Documentos, no. 34).

The author divides the Portuguese territory into three physiographically well-defined zones according to climate, grouping the meteorological stations within each of these zones, making it possible to compare the influence of the climate in the three zones and its relation to agriculture, soil and vegetation.

A tale of two states: ecology and the political economy of inequality on the island of Roti.
See item no. 134.

Filling the gap: delimiting the Australia–Indonesia maritime boundary.
See item no. 283.

Geology

35 The geology of Portugese Timor.
Michael Geoffrey Audley-Charles. London: Geological Society of London, 1968. 76p. maps. bibliog. (Memoir, no. 4).

This is a revised doctoral thesis and is unfortunately stuck with some of the tedium and opaqueness that often characterize such works. However, the thoroughness of the work cannot be denied, and it is an important reference work for those interested in the development of Timor's oil industry in the wake of the Timor Gap treaty.

36 The geology of Indonesia.
Reinout Willem van Bemmelen. The Hague, The Netherlands: Government Printing Office, 1949. 2 vols.

This exhaustive work, despite its age, still represents the best source of general geological information on West Timor, and should be the starting point for any further research. Volume 1a covers general geology, volume 1b is a portfolio and volume 2 is a survey of economically important geological formations throughout the archipelago, including East Timor.

37 Basalt geochemistry as a test of the tectonic models of Timor.
R.F. Berry, G.A. Jenner. *Journal of the Geological Society* (London), vol. 139, no. 5 (Sept. 1982), p. 593–664. bibliog. map.

The tectonic origin of Timor by the collision of the Sahul and Sunda plates is widely accepted but the detailed structure of the island is a subject of contention. There is active disagreement over the style of deformation recorded in the geology of Timor and of the origin of many of the major stratigraphic units. The authors deal with the last problem.

38 **Sobre o conhecimento petrográfico da ilha de Ataúro (Província de Timor).** (On the petrographic knowledge of the island of Atauro [Timor Province].)
José António Neves Brak-Lamy. *Garcia de Orta*, vol. 4, no. 4 (1956), p. 581–88. bibliog.

This paper lists, in a dry academic style, the petrographic and chemical characteristics of certain rock samples obtained from the small island of Atauro off the north coast of East Timor.

39 **Contribution à la connaisance de la géologie de la province portugaise de Timor.** (A contribution to the understanding of the geology of the Portuguese province of Timor.)
Robert Gageonnet, Marcel Lemoine. Lisbon: Ministério do Ultramar, Junta de Investigações do Ultramar, 1958. 136p. map. bibliog. (Estudos, Ensaios e Documentos, no. 48).

This French-language report covers the whole of East Timor except for Atauro. The authors study the stratigraphy and tectonics of East Timor in detail, and then attempt to correlate it stratigraphically and tectonically with the Indonesian part of the island. They recognize a deep tectonic element, and an overthrusted complex formed of various elements of exotic origin, concluding that Neogene and Pleistocene elements were deposited after the overthrusting.

40 **Geologia do encrave de Ocussi (Província de Timor).** (The geology of Oecussi enclave [Timor Province].)
João de Azeredo Leme, António Vasconcelos Teixeira Pinto Coelho. *Garcia de Orta*, vol. 10, no. 3 (1962), p. 553–66. map. bibliog.

This account (also to be found in *Estudos Agronómicos*, vol. 3, no. 3 [July 1962], p. 119–32), is divided into two parts: the first part, besides some general features such as climate and morphology, deals with the regional geology, while the second part is especially devoted to petrographic and chemical studies. The whole is illustrated with some relevant photographs of the landscape and some rock sections.

Fauna

41 **Mammals of southeast Asia.**
Earl of Cranbrook. Singapore: Oxford University Press, 1991. 2nd ed.
96p. bibliog. map.
Originally published as *Riches of the wild: land mammals of southeast Asia* in 1987, this
book begins by explaining how the region's past geological history and present climate
have favoured the evolution of an exceptionally rich fauna of some 660 species. The six
subsequent chapters, beautifully illustrated with coloured plates by Cdr. A.M. Hughes,
show the diversity of these mammals, group by group. A checklist, including Timor, is
appended.

42 **List of land mammals of New Guinea, Celebes and adjacent islands,
1758–1952.**
E.M.O. Laurie, J.E. Hill. London: British Museum, 1954. 175p. map.
The coverage of this useful list extends from Lombok in the west to the Solomon
Islands in the east. All recent wild taxa are listed: 351 species in 122 genera in 23
families in 8 orders, and the approximate range of each taxon is given. A gazetteer of
the type localities and some obscure collecting localities lists 878 entries. It does,
appear, however, to be incomplete for rodents and bats.

43 **Birds of Timor and Sumba.**
Ernest Mayr. *Bulletin of the American Museum of Natural History*, no.
83 (1944), p. 123–94. maps.
At the time of writing 137 breeding and 31 migratory bird species were known in
Timor. Taxonomic notes are given and there is a short discussion on the effect of
altitude on distribution patterns in Timor. Zoogeography is discussed under the
following headings: notes on the zoogeography of Timor and Sumba; the faunal
components of the bird fauna of Timor; endemism on Timor; the colonization by birds
of Timor; regional zoogeography, land bridges and dispersal faculties and the criteria
for land bridges.

44 **Land mammals of Indonesia.**
   W. Veevers-Carter.   Jakarta: PT Intermasa, 1979. 115p. map. bibliog.
Arranged according to taxonomic order, there are page-long descriptions of forty-eight mammals, giving English, Indonesian and Latin names. There is also a list of mammals allowing them to be placed according to island or island group, including Nusa Tenggara.

A naturalist's wanderings in the eastern archipelago.
See item no. 13.

The Malay archipelago: the land of the orang-utan and the bird of paradise. A narrative of travel with studies of man and nature.
See item no. 17.

Flora

45 Prodomus floræ timorensis.
Compiled in the Botanical Department of the British Museum: J.
Britten, W. Fawcett, H.N. Ridley, W. Carruthers. In: *A naturalist's
wanderings in the Eastern archipelago*. By Henry O. Forbes. Singapore:
Oxford University Press, 1989. p. 497–523. (Oxford in Asia Hardback
Reprints).

Between December 1882 and May 1883 Forbes travelled through East Timor collecting
plants for a new herbarium of Timor. He describes the route he took and the different
places at which the collections were made, as well as pointing out the Timorese
herbaria extant at that time. Any new species that were found are listed.

46 Esboço histórico do sândalo no Timor Portugûes. (An historical outline
of sandalwood in Portuguese Timor.)
Ruy Cinatti Vaz Monteiro Gomes.   Lisbon: Ministério das Colónias,
Junta de Investigações Coloniais, 1950. 31p.

An outline of the sandalwood tree (*Santalum album*): botanical description,
geographical distribution, ecology, silvicultural characteristics and exploitation. It also
mentions the importance of sandalwood in the history of Portugal's presence in Timor
and the problems of continued production at the time of writing.

47 Explorações botânicas em Timor. (Botanical explorations in Timor.)
Ruy Cinatti Vaz Monteiro Gomes.   Lisbon: Ministério das Colónias,
Junta de Investigações Coloniais, 1950. 64p. bibliog. (Estudos, Ensaios e
Documentos, no. 4).

A chronological account, together with short bibliographical notes, of those who
visited Timor and brought back botanical material. A short account is also given of the
botanical activities of the author during his time in Timor as secretary to the governor,
1946–47.

48 **Reconhecimento preliminar das formações florestais no Timor Português.** (A preliminary survey of forest types in Portuguese Timor.) Ruy Cinatti Vaz Monteiro Gomes. Lisbon: Ministério das Colónias, Junta de Investigações Coloniais, 1950. 80p. map. bibliog. (Estudos, Ensaios e Documentos, no. 5).

The author's two years as secretary to the governor did not allow him to undertake a systemic survey of Timorese vegetation types but he was able to formulate a definition of the principle types of forest formations to be found.

49 **Vegetables of the Dutch East Indies.** Jacob Jonas Ochse. Amsterdam: J. Ascher, 1931. 1,005p.

This classic work, reprinted in 1975, with amended scientific plant names and illustrations, covers the tubers, bulbs, rhizomes, herbs and spices and other edible vegetables of southeast Asia. Entries include the botany, usage and sketches of the plants.

50 **Flora Malesiana, 1948–54.** C.G.G.J. van Steenis. Jakarta: Nordhoff-Kolff, 1948. (Series 1, Spermatophyta, vols. 1–10; Pteridophyta, vol. 1–).

This, the major current flora of the archipelago, is part of an ongoing study by botanists specializing in the flora of the Indonesian world.

51 **Tree flora of Indonesia: check list for Bali, Nusa Tenggara and Timor.** Edited by T.C. Whitmore, I.G.M. Tantra, U. Sutisna. Bogor, Indonesia: Ministry of Forestry, Forestry Research and Development Centre, 1989. 119p.

Indonesia does not yet have a comprehensive account of its forest trees. This checklist is one of a planned set of six which, it is hoped, will cover the whole country. The list is arranged alphabetically according to family. Within every family are the genera which have at least one big tree species in the region and all the recorded species for every genus are listed. The names of small trees, shrubs, climbers and herbs are included in brackets. For every species the following information is given: scientific name; references relevant to Indonesia; size; height and diameter; a very brief note of habitat and type of forest and elevation above sea level; geographical range from west to east, and a note of any important uses. There is a single alphabetical sequence of all the recorded vernacular names for most provinces.

A naturalist's wanderings in the eastern archipelago.
See item no. 13.

Flora

The Malay archipelago: the land of the orang-utan and the bird of paradise. A narrative of travel with studies of man and nature.
See item no. 17.

Le savoir botanique des Bunaq: percevoir et classer dans le Haut Lamaknen (Timor, Indonésie). (Botanical knowledge among the Bunak: perception and classification in Upper Lamaknen [Timor, Indonesia].)
See item no. 109.

Ethnomédecine et ethnoscience: nosologie et etiologie chez les Bunaq de Timor (Indonésie). (Ethnomedicine and ethnoscience: nosology and etiology among the Bunak of Timor, Indonesia.)
See item no. 110.

Grasses of Portuguese Timor and information about their fodder value.
See item no. 294.

Archaeology and Prehistory

52 **Mollusca in Indonesian archaeological research.**
Emily A. Glover. *Indonesia Circle*, no. 40 (Jan. 1986), p. 33–45.
bibliog. map.

In this well-presented and lucid article the author provides mollusc evidence from two coastal cave sites in East Timor and Sulawesi to reveal past patterns of foraging, tool and ornament manufacture, long-term climatic stability and changing sea-levels from the late Pleistocene to about 2,000 years ago. The Timorese today are not happy to go to sea and the absence of fish remains at the site show that this was probably the case at that time too.

53 **Archaeology in East Timor, 1966–1967.**
Ian C. Glover.   Canberra: Department of Prehistory, Research School of Pacific Studies, Australian National University, 1986. 241p. map.
(Terra Australis, no. 11).

This monograph, an edited version of the author's 1972 PhD dissertation, details excavations carried out between 1966 and 1967 at four cave sites in the northern part of East Timor. Now pre-eminent in the field of Timorese archaeology, Glover focuses on the timing of the initial Pleistocene settlement of Australia and upon technical innovations appearing in Australian stone industries early in the Holocene era.

54 **The late stone age in eastern Indonesia.**
Ian C. Glover.   In: *Prehistoric Indonesia: a reader.* Edited by Pieter van de Velde. Dordrecht, The Netherlands; Cinnaminson, New Jersey: Foris Publications, 1984. (Verhandelingen van het Koninklijk Instituut voor Taal-, Land- en Volkenkunde, no. 104).

The author uses evidence from East Timor, south Sulawesi and the Talaud Islands to conclude that the area was settled by man some time in the Upper Pleistocene. There is a summary of the results of his excavations carried out on the edge of the dry northern coastal plain near Baucau and in the central mountains of East Timor. This material also appeared in *Indonesia Circle*, no. 12 (March 1977), p. 6–20, and *World Archaeology*, vol. 9, no. 1 (June 1977), p. 42–61, including maps and bibliography.

55 Pleistocene flaked stone tools from Timor and Flores.
Ian C. Glover, Emily A. Glover. *Mankind*, vol. 7, no. 3 (June 1970), p. 188–90.

A study of seven choppers and scrapers from West Timor and Flores kept at a university in Kupang. Collected as surface finds on Pleistocene gravels, where the remains of *stegadon* were also discovered, and similar in appearance to tools from Pacitan in Java, they suggest a Pleistocene origin.

56 Prehistoric research in Timor.
Ian C. Glover. In: *Aboriginal man and environment in Australia*. Edited by D.J. Mulvaney, J. Golson. Canberra: Australian National University Press, 1971, p. 158–81. map. bibliog.

The author here offers a fact-filled, well-illustrated distillation of what is known about Timorese archaeology. Timor is important for archaeological research because of its proximity to Australia, allowing archaeologists to date the arrival of man in Australia and the spread of pottery, horticulture and domesticated animals into eastern Indonesia and Melanesia.

57 Radiocarbon dates from Portuguese Timor.
Ian C. Glover. *Archaeology and Physical Anthropology in Oceania*, no. 4 (July 1969), p. 107–12. bibliog.

A brief, well-documented description of the first radiocarbon dating for eastern Indonesia. A very important work for dating the phases of human Timorese inhabitation and its direct bearing on Melanesian cultural history.

History

General

58 **Fidalgos in the Far East, 1550–1770.**
Charles Ralph Boxer.   Hong Kong: Oxford University Press, 1968. 2nd
ed. 298p. bibliog.
Chapter 11, 'Turbulent Timor', is of particular interest, but the work as a whole
exhibits the author's ability to draw widely from Dutch and Portuguese sources from
the seventeenth and eighteenth century, making him one of the leading contributors to
the history of Timor.

59 **Southeast Asia's second front: the power struggle in the Malay
archipelago.**
Arnold C. Brackman.   London: Pall Mall, 1966. 129p.
This work has an interesting note on Indonesian intentions in Portuguese Timor in the
early 1960s and the declaration of a United Republic of Timor in 1963.

60 **The great lord rests at the centre: the paradox of powerlessness in
European–Timorese relations.**
James J. Fox.   *Canberra Anthropology*, vol. 9, no. 2 (1982), p. 22–33.
bibliog.
In 1642 the Portuguese destroyed the ritual confederation of Timor and its centre
Wehali, on the south coast. This marked the beginning of 150 years of struggle for
power between them and the Dutch, each represented by local factions of *Topasses*.
The authority of the Great Lord of Wehali survived and remained intact for another
250 years. According to the author, this resilience was due to the conceptualization of
the Great Lord of Wehali as the female principle of authority, spiritual in nature.
Temporal power had been given away to Lords in satellite centres who embodied the
male principle. Allegiance to foreign powers in the periphery did not signify a break
with the past.

61 **Religious and economic aspects of Portuguese–Indonesian relations 1509–1641.**
Sartono Kartodirdjo. *Studia*, no. 29 (April 1970), p. 175–96. bibliog.
Not of specific reference to Timor but, for those interested in Timor in relation to the archipelago as a whole, this work is an excellent study of the Portuguese presence in the archipelago between 1500 and 1640. The author argues that much of the previous work is Euro-centric, bearing 'a strong patriotic and religious bias, a sense of Portuguese mission in Asia and an intolerance and suspicion of Muslims'.

62 **The secret discovery of Australia: Portuguese ventures 250 years before Captain Cook.**
Kenneth Gordon McIntyre. Sydney: Picador, 1982. rev. and abridged ed'. 236p. bibliog.
An intriguing book which claims that the Portuguese did not just stop at Timor, but made the 500 kilometre crossing of the Timor Sea and discovered Australia 250 years before Captain Cook. The major piece of evidence is a set of Portuguese maps known as the Dieppe Maps. Much of the book is taken up with their presentation and interpretation. The discussion is fascinating and is illustrated with many maps and diagrams.

63 **Colonial rivalries in Timor.**
William Burton Sowash. *The Far Eastern Quarterly*, vol. 8, no. 3 (May 1948), p. 226–35. map.
The core of this article is a very useful overview of the island as a whole and how it became split in half. The petty, small-scale incursions of much of the military encounters between the representatives of the Dutch and Portuguese administrations left each territory dotted with enclaves belonging to the other power. The status of many of these disputed areas was only sorted out early this century.

East Timor

64 **Timor: da ocupação japonesa a ocupação indonesia.** (Timor: from the Japanese occupation to Indonesian occupation.)
Filipe Themudo Barata. *Independência*, no. 5 (1987), p. 3–8.
Provides a personal narrative by a former Portuguese governor of Timor on the contemporary history of East Timor, noting the occupation by Japan in 1942, threats from Indonesia in 1959, the Goa crisis in 1961, the Portuguese revolution in 1974, the civil war and the Indonesian invasion beginning in 1975.

65 **Francisco Vieira de Figueiredo: a Portuguese merchant-adventurer in southeast Asia, 1624–1667.**
Charles Ralph Boxer. The Hague, The Netherlands: Nijhoff, 1967.
53p. bibliog. (Verhandelingen van het Koninklijk Instituut voor Taal-, Land- en Volkenkunde, no. 52).
As with all of Boxer's work this short work is thoroughly researched from many sources and lucidly written. Many of the original documents are presented in nearly fifty pages of appendices. De Figueiredo, by forging links with the *Topasses*, can be attributed with assuring Portugal a lengthy presence in Timor.

66 **Portuguese Timor: a rough island story, 1515–1960.**
Charles Ralph Boxer. *History Today*, vol. 10, no. 5 (May 1960), p. 349–55. map.
Based on Portuguese sources this account deals with East Timorese history up until 1700 but very little thereafter. The article was written when Timor was in the news again at a time of Indonesian expansionism.

67 **A ordem de São Domingos e as origens de Timor.** (The Dominican Order and the origins of Timor.)
João Diogo Alarcão Carvalho Branco. *Independência*, no. 5 (1987), p. 35–47.
Describes the important role that Dominican missionaries played in the Portuguese colonization of Timor during the sixteenth and seventeenth centuries, noting the rôle of specific missionaries and their impact on the region.

68 **Indonesia: an alternative history.**
Malcolm Caldwell, Ernst Utrecht. Sydney: Alternative Publishing Co-operative, 1979. 192p. map.
These prominent left-wing authors cite the aggression used by Indonesia in the annexation of East Timor as an example of what the authors call the 'centrifugal forces at work in the country, the incompetence of the Indonesian military and moreover the occurences that have taken place long after measures were adopted to produce a modicum of efficiency, decease of corruption and national unity'. Poor print quality and a large number of printing errors make reading difficult.

69 **Timor: subsídios para a sua história.** (Timor: contributions to its history.)
Gonçalo Pimenta de Castro. Lisbon: Ministério das Colónias, 1944. 218p. map.
It was popular among ex-administrators of East Timor to write their memoires of their time in the province. Some have become invaluable to the understanding of the history of Timor, for example, the work of Leitão (q.v.), others are interesting as personal recollections. This is worth mentioning for its arrangement of contents according to governor.

70 **East Timor: exchange and political hierarchy at the time of the European discoveries.**
Shepard Forman. In: *Economic exchange and social interaction in Southeast Asia, perspectives from prehistory, history and ethnography.* Edited by Karl Hutterer. Ann Arbor, Michigan: Center For South and Southeast Asian Studies, University of Michigan, 1977, p. 97–111. map. (Michigan Papers on South and Southeast Asia, no. 13).

The author maintains that the history of the Makassai people of East Timor provides some possible insights into the processes of political integration both before and during the Portuguese presence. He describes the political and economic system in the Lesser Sunda Islands at the time of the European arrival and the re-ordering which took place in the course of Dutch and Portuguese competition for commercial hegemony in the region in the seventeenth and eighteenth centuries, the relative neglect of the Lesser Sunda Islands following the Dutch defeat of the Portuguese and the subsequent marginalization of the commercial economy in Timor and the extension of the Portuguese administration bureaucracy in Timor in the late nineteenth century.

71 **The Timor Problem – I, II, III.**
Peter Hastings. *Australian Outlook*, vol. 29, no. 1 (April 1975), p. 18–33; vol. 29, no. 2 (Aug. 1975), p. 180–97; vol. 29, no. 3 (Dec. 1975), p. 323–34.

A series of very good articles covering the East Timorese economy, social welfare and Australia's views on the province throughout this century including some references to the First World War.

72 **Sejarah Timor Timur.** (The history of East Timor.)
A.B. Lapian, Paramita Abdurachman. *Berita Antropologi*, vol. 11, no. 36 (Jan.–March 1980), p. 9–36. map.

This article briefly considers both the prehistory of East Timor and the kingdom of Wehali. But, despite its title, the article is basically a discussion of both the Dutch presence in the island between 1643 and 1949 and the Portuguese presence between 1660 and 1975.

73 **Os portugueses em Solor e Timor de 1515 a 1702.** (The Portuguese in Solor and Timor from 1515 to 1702.)
Humberto Leitão. Lisbon: Tip. LCGG, 1948. 303p.

This Portuguese naval officer, with a record of long service in Timor, conducted the research for this book on the relevant documents preserved in the Arquivo Histórico Colónial at Lisbon. It is well-illustrated with a number of sketch maps, and is of particular interest for its exhaustive analysis of the voyage of António de Abreu past the island early in the sixteenth century.

74 **Timor, quatro séculos de colonização portuguesa.** (Timor: four centuries
of Portuguese colonization.)
José Simões Martinho. Porto: Editora Livraria Progredior, 1943. 306p.
map. bibliog.
The introduction notes that, through this work, the author hopes to contribute to a spirit
of colonialism. This may account for its style, a sort of handbook for future
administrators. Martinho served for nearly twenty-five years with the Portuguese army
in Timor, and this is therefore largely a military history with a large section on
relations with the Dutch. There is also a brief ethnography and a short Tetun
grammar.

75 **Timor Português, 1515–1796: contribuição para a sua história.**
(Portuguese Timor, 1515–1796: a contribution to its history.)
Artur Teodoro de Matos. Lisbon: Faculdade de Letras da
Universidade de Lisboa, Instituto Histórico Infante Dom Henrique,
1974. 208p. map. bibliog.
For the period between the sixteenth and eighteenth century this is the best single
volume on Portuguese rule yet available. Supplementing an intimate knowledge of the
published sources with other primary materials, the author weaves a skilful summary,
rich in illustrative detail, of the early voyages of discovery, and Timor's conquest by
sword and cross.

76 **Timor na história de Portugal.** (Timor in Portuguese history.)
Luna de Oliveira. vols. 1 & 2: Lisbon: Agência Geral das Colónias,
1949, 1950; vol. 3: Agência Geral do Ultramar, 1952. 310p.
Much of the early material is covered in other works, but these volumes are
particularly strong on administrative matters. Volume three is noteworthy for carrying
the only substantial mention of Timor during the First World War. Volume four,
covering the period 1918–50, appears to have been prepared and then suppressed,
suffering the same fate as the report of the Second World War by the governor of
Portuguese Timor at the time, Manuel de Abreu Ferreira de Carvalho.

77 **Da campanha de 1726 às pedras de Cailaco.** (The campaign of 1726 to
the rocky shores of Cailaco.)
Manuel A. Ribeiro Rodrigues. *Independência*, no. 5 (1987), p. 14–18.
Rodrigues describes a Portuguese campaign to crush the rebellion in the kingdom of
Cailaco in Timor. The rocky natural defences of the kingdom were not sufficient to
stop the military expedition.

West Timor

78 **Perjuangan kemerdekaan Indonesia di Nusa Tenggara Timur.** (The fight
for Indonesian independence in Nusa Tenggara Timur.)
I.H. Doko. Jakarta: Balai Pustaka, 1981. 280p. bibliog. map.

The author was formative in the creation of Indonesian nationalism in the region
during the 1930s and 1940s. This is partly a factual history of that period and partly
personal recollections, including some valuable details about the cultural and political
organizations Timorsch Verbond, Timorsch Jongeren and Perserikatan Kebangsaan
Timor.

79 **Sejarah daerah Nusa Tenggara Timur.** (The history of Nusa Tenggara
Timur.)
Department of Education and Culture. Jakarta: Republic of Indonesia,
Department of Education and Culture, 1977. 147p.

This book covers the prehistoric period and the history of the region up to the
twentieth century. It relates the history of Alor, Belagar, Sikka and Manggarai, and
provides extensive details about the emergence of the nationalist movements and the
course of the struggle for independence from Dutch colonialism.

80 **Sejarah kebangkitan nasional daerah Nusa Tenggara Timur.** (The history
of national development in Nusa Tenggara Timur.)
Department of Education and Culture. Jakarta: Republic of Indonesia,
Department of Education and Culture, 1978. 103p.

Describes political and economic developments from the end of the nineteenth century
to the landing of the Japanese in 1942. It provides detailed information on the effects
of the economic crisis and the situation of the political parties after their foundation.

81 **Sejarah perlawanan terhadap imperialisme dan kolonialisme di Nusa
Tenggara Timur.** (The history of resistance to colonialism and
imperialism in Nusa Tenggara Timur.)
Department of Education and Culture. Jakarta: Republic of Indonesia,
Department of Education and Culture, 1982. 196p. map.

The author describes here the historical resistance to Dutch colonial rule in Timor,
Flores, Savu and Roti.

Incursions upon Wehali: a modern history of an ancient empire.
See item no. 148.

Second World War

82 **Funo: guerra em Timor.** (Funo: war in Timor.)
Carlos Cal Brandão. Lisbon: Perspectivas e Realidades, 1987. 4th ed.
152p.
The author, a *deportado*, became a leading lawyer in Portuguese Timor. He cooperated with the Allied forces, and was among those evacuated to Australia where he became a translator. He acted as an interpreter for a representative of the Australian Department of External affairs at the Japanese surrender in Dili. This is a record of his experiences.

83 **Timor entre invasores, 1941–1945.** (Timor between invaders,
1941–1945.)
Maria de Graça Bretes. Lisbon: Livros Horizonte, 1989. 50p. map.
bibliog.
This brief monograph, with lengthy documentary annexes, deals with the Australian and Dutch invasion of East Timor and the ensuing Japanese invasion. There is a discussion of some of the internal and external factors leading to the invasion and some of the diplomatic efforts with regard to Timor, especially the return of Portuguese sovereignty after the war.

84 **Tata Mai Lau: Timor contra o Japão.** (Tata Mai Lau: Timor against
Japan.)
Francisco Garcia de Brito. Lisbon: Iniciativas Editonais, 1977. 293p.
The author was attached to the headquarters of the Portuguese military administration in Dili. During the Japanese occupation he was interned in the zone of concentration and wrote this book directly after the war from notes made at that time. It is a much more personal account than those of other Portuguese officials.

85 **Independent Company: the 2/2 and 2/4 Australian Independent
companies in Portuguese Timor, 1941–1943.**
Bernard J. Callinan. Melbourne, Australia: Heinemann, 1953. 235p.
maps.
The author landed in Timor in December 1941 as part of the 2/2 Australian Independent Company, and here describes the period between then and the evacuation of the Australian troops in early 1943, especially the mountain guerilla warfare campaign launched against the Japanese by the Australians. A paperback version of the book was published by William Heinemann, (Richmond, Australia, 1984) the only alterations being the title-page, viz., *Independent Company: the Australian army in Portuguese Timor 1941–1943* by Bernard Callinan.

86 **Vida e morte em Timor durante a segunda guerra mundial.** (Life and
death in Timor during the Second World War.)
José dos Santos Carvalho. Lisbon: Livraria Portugal, 1972. 209p. map.
The author, a doctor, arrived in Portuguese Timor at the end of December 1940, acting as health delegate for the central and eastern parts of the colony. In August 1943 he became head of the colony's health services. This book encompasses the

events from his arrival until the end of the Second World War and reports on the colony's health services for the years 1943–45

87 **Timor . . . II: the world of Dr. Evatt.**
W.D. Forsyth. *New Guinea and Australia, the Pacific and Southeast Asia*, vol. 10, no. 1 (June 1975), p. 31–37.

This account rather drily records Australia's concern at the apparent lack of security in Portuguese Timor in the run up to the Second World War. Dr. Evatt was the Australian Minister for External Affairs at the time, and tried to set up a zone of defence including Timor. The in-depth account of the Japanese surrender on Timor is enlivened by 'a freezing night flight during which one of the four motors caught fire over Arnhem Land.'

88 **Wartime Portuguese Timor: the Azores connection.**
Geoffrey C. Gunn. Clayton, Australia: Monash University, 1986. 19p. bibliog. (Centre of Southeast Asian Studies Working Papers, no. 50).

Unlike the case of the Netherlands East Indies, where the colonial restoration was opposed both militarily and politically, no challenge arose in Portuguese Timor to the restoration of colonial power in the post-surrender period. According to the author the Portuguese Prime Minister, Dr. António de Oliveira Salazar was able to skilfully lay claim upon Anglo-American support for the maintenance of the Portuguese empire (Timor included) in exchange for allied access to the mid-Atlantic base facilities on the Portuguese-controlled Azores Islands.

89 **De strijd op Timor.** (The struggle in Timor.)
C. van den Hoogenband, L. Schotborgh. In: *Nederlands-Indië contra Japan. Deel VI: de strijd op Ambon, Timor en Sumatra.* By C. van den Hoogenband, L. Schotborgh. The Hague, The Netherlands: Defence Department, 1959, p. 24–60. map.

This is the detailed official Dutch account of events during the Second World War. It notes Dutch concern at Japanese interest in Portuguese Timor and the subsequent invasion. It describes the effortless Japanese invasion of Timor in February 1942 and the guerilla warfare carried on in both East and West Timor by Dutch and Australian troops.

90 **Quando Timor foi notícia: memorias.** (When Timor was news: memoires.)
Cacilda dos Santos Oliveira Liberato. Braga, Portugal: Editoria Pax, 1972. 205p. map.

The author, arrived in Portuguese Timor in September 1936, where her husband was a civil servant. He was killed in a massacre at Aileu in October 1942, but she was able to escape with her children. These are her experiences and appear to be countered by *Também quero depor sobre Timor, 1941–1946* (I also wish to bear witness to Timor, 1941–1946) by António de Sousa Santos, published in Lourenço Marques, 1973. 82p.

91 **Resistance in Timor.**
Lionel Wigmore. In: *The Japanese thrust.* By Lionel Wigmore.
Canberra: Australian War Memorial, 1957, p. 466-94. map. (Australia
in the war of 1939–45, vol. 4).

A highly detailed, virtually day-to-day account of the situation at the Dutch end of the
island, the invasion of Dili and the actions of Australian commandos in Portuguese
Timor. There are a number of personal recollections used in the text, making it a
highly readable piece.

92 **Timor 1942: Australian commandos at war with the Japanese.**
Christopher C.H. Wray. Melbourne: Mandarin Australia, 1987. 190p.
map.

The most complete book to exist on the Australian actions in Portuguese Timor. The
author's father served in Timor, and he has brought together material from published
and unpublished sources in order to present a broader history of Australian military
operations in Timor than has previously been available. For a guide to some of the
people mentioned in the book see item no. 347.

Timor during the first and second world wars: some notes on sources.
See item no. 347.

Timorese Peoples

General

93 **The people and languages of Timor.**
Arthur Capell. *Oceania*, vol. 14, no. 3 (March 1944), p. 191–219; vol. 14, no. 4 (June 1944), p. 311–37; vol. 15, no. 1 (Sept. 1944), p. 19–48. map. bibliog.
Despite its age this solidly researched series of articles remains one of the best introductions to the Timorese people and their languages available in English. The first part is a general outline and an introduction to the ethnology of the island, the second part introduces the reader to the languages of Timor with a comparative vocabulary of the main languages. Part three is rather more specialized; a comparative text in the languages of Kupang, Vaikenu, Western and Eastern Tetun, Mambai, Galoli, Waimaka and Atoni.

94 **Gentio de Timor.** (The people of Timor.)
Armando Pinto Corrêa. Lisbon: Lucas, 1934. 347p. map. bibliog.
The author served as an administrator in Baucau in Portuguese Timor. He wrote prolifically of his experiences in the province and, as with his other works, this book is entertaining and informative. Designed for the general Portuguese public, it is a general ethnography of Timor, thorough without being too detailed or scholarly. About half of the book deals specifically with the Baucau region.

95 **Timor: ritos e mitos atauros.** (Timor: rites and myths of Atauro.)
Jorge Barros Duarte. Lisbon: Ministério de Educação, Instituto de Cultura e Lingua Portuguesa, 1984. 307p. bibliog.
The island of Atauro lies seventeen miles off the coast of East Timor, directly north of Dili. It rises sharply from the sea; its 140 square kilometres reaching 960 metres at their highest point. This work, the only substantial work on the people of the island,

deals primarily with the religious aspects of their life, but also includes many details of their day-to-day existence.

96 **The flow of life: essays on eastern Indonesia.**
Edited by James J. Fox. Cambridge, Massachusetts: Harvard University Press, 1980. 372p. map. bibliog. (Harvard Studies in Cultural Anthropology, no. 2).

The essays in this volume form both a collaborative consideration of a number of societies on the islands of eastern Indonesia, including Timor, and a critical commentary of a classic work in Dutch anthropology which first brought the region to the attention of western anthropologists as a field of research: F.A.E. van Wouden's *Types of social structure in eastern Indonesia* (q.v.). Six of the essays deal specifically with Timor, covering societies in both the east and the west.

97 **Timor-Roti.**
David Hicks. In: *Ethnic groups of insular southeast Asia, vol. 1: Indonesia, Andaman Islands and Madagascar.* Edited by Frank M. LeBar. New Haven, Connecticut: Human Relations Area Files Press, 1972, p. 97–98. bibliog.

This general introduction covers the Eastern Tetun, Atoni, Helong, Rotinese and Ndaonese under the headings of general information, location, settlement patterns, economy, kin groups, descent, marriage and family, political and social organization and religious systems.

98 **Types of social structure in eastern Indonesia.**
F.A.E. van Wouden, translated from the Dutch by Rodney Needham. The Hague, The Netherlands: Martinus Nijhoff, 1968. 166p. bibliog. (Koninklijk Instituut voor Taal-, Land- en Volkenkunde Translation Series, no. 2).

Submitted by van Wouden as his doctoral dissertation at Leiden in 1935, this has become the classic work in Dutch anthropology that defined the islands in question – Sumba in the west, Timor in the south, the Kei islands in the east and Halmahera in the north – as a field of ethnological study of major theoretical interest. He stated that in the area of study exclusive cross-cousin marriage (a man may only marry a mother's brother's daughter) occupied a position of eminent importance. His work shows that this marriage custom is the pivot on which turns the activity of the social groups, the clans. Timorese society is organized according to their mythological beliefs, and through this there emerges the essential interconnection and similarity of the human and the cosmic. Chapter four refers this proposition directly to the case of Timor, detailing its social structure, both historically and at the time of writing, relating it to the mythological explanations of the social structure told by the Timorese themselves.

Bibliography of Indonesian peoples and cultures.
See item no. 342.

Atoni and Helong

99 **Atoni.**
In: *Ethnic groups of insular southeast Asia, vol. 1: Indonesia, Andaman Islands and Madagascar.* Edited by Frank M. LeBar. New Haven, Connecticut: Human Relations Area Files Press, 1972, p. 103–05. bibliog.

Covers the orientation, settlement patterns and housing, traditional economy, marriage, kin groups and sociopolitical organization of the Atoni people of West Timor. It is dated in that it refers to the former administrative unit in West Timor, the *kefettoran.*

100 **Atoni kin categories and conventional behaviour.**
Clark E. Cunningham. *Bijdragen tot de Taal-, Land- en Volkenkunde,* vol. 123, no. 1 (1967), p. 53–70. bibliog.

A detailed and scholarly discussion of Atoni kin terminology, the variations and combinations of various categories with Atoni society.

101 **Categories of descent groups in a Timor village.**
Clark E. Cunningham. *Oceania,* vol. 37, no. 1 (Sept. 1966), p. 13–21. bibliog.

Describes the two complementary categories of descent groups whose members are citizens of any Atoni settlement. Each is characterized by its original settlement and subsequent marriage into the area, reducing the ties between descent groups to a simple local pattern.

102 **Order and change in the Atoni diarchy.**
Clark E. Cunningham. *Southwestern Journal of Anthropology,* vol. 21, no. 4 (1965), p. 359–82. maps. bibliog.

This paper describes the relationship between ideology and organization in a particular Atoni princedom and the problems which arose when this princedom was confronted with a colonial monarchic and bureaucratic system in the twentieth century.

103 **Soba: an Atoni village of West Timor.**
Clark E. Cunningham. In: *Villages in Indonesia.* Edited by R.M. Koentjaraningrat. Ithaca, New York: Cornell University Press, 1967, p. 63–89. map.

Based on fieldwork conducted between 1959–61, this is an accomplished brief introduction to the lives of the Atoni, who numbered about 300,000 at the time of writing. Cunningham describes their environment and location, subsistence economies, property rights, arts and crafts, kinship relations, social stratification, ceremonial activities, religious beliefs, village administration and leadership. Written just a decade after Indonesian independence it concludes with the impact of that event on the traditional lifestyle of the Atoni. An Indonesian translation was also produced under the title 'Soba, sebuah desa Atoni di Timor-Barat' in *Masyarakat desa di Indonesia masa ini* (edited by R.M. Koentjaraningrat. Jakarta: Yayasan Badan Penerbit Fakultas Ekonomi, Universitas Indonesia. p. 225–52).

104 **Helong.**
James J. Fox.   In: *Ethnic groups of insular southeast Asia, vol. 1*:
Indonesia, Andaman Islands and Madagascar. Edited by Frank M.
LeBar. New Haven, Connecticut: Human Relations Area Files Press,
1972, p. 105. bibliog.

One of the only descriptions of this small community living in the very west of Timor,
around Kupang and on the island of Semau, this is a good general introduction, very
much in the standard LeBar formula.

105 **The symbolic classification of the Atoni of Timor.**
Herman Gerrit Schulte Nordholt.   In: *The flow of life: essays on
eastern Indonesia.* Edited by James J. Fox. Cambridge, Massachusetts:
Harvard University Press, 1980, p. 231–47.

This scholarly discussion of important social linkages in Atoni society, with specific
case studies, is only for those initiated with the broader context.

106 **The political system of the Atoni of Timor.**
Herman Gerrit Schulte Nordholt, translated by M.J.L. van Yperen.
The Hague, The Netherlands: Martinus Nijhoff, 1971. 479p. maps.
bibliog. (Verhandelingen van het Koninklijk Instituut voor Taal-,
Land- en Volkenkunde, no. 60).

This is a reworked doctoral thesis submitted to the Free University, Amsterdam and
originally published in Dutch as *Het politieke systeem van de Atoni van Timor*
(Driebergen, The Netherlands: Offsetdruk Van Manen, 1966). It is a readable and
informative outline of the world of the Atoni, including a description of the rites
accompanying the agricultural cycle which is the basis for the political system. Mention
is made of the kinship system and religion. The analysis of the political system consists
of an historical outline, an analysis of the different political systems of the princedoms
and a summary of the Timorese political system in general. By way of conclusion the
author covers the place that the Atoni system of life occupies in Indonesian culture as a
whole.

Proeve van een Timorese grammatica. (An interim Timorese grammar.)
See item no. 159.

Agricultures timoraises. (Timorese agriculture.)
See item no. 287.

**The development of traditional agricultural practices in western Timor: from
the ritual control of consumer goods production to the political control of
prestige goods.**
See item no. 288.

Head hunting in Timor and its historical implication.
See item no. 307.

**Migration of Timorese groups and the question of the *kase metan* or overseas
black foreigners.**
See item no. 308.

Nai Tirans en Nai Besi in komische huwelijksrelatie met de krokodil. (Nai Tirans en Nai Besi in an amusing marriage with the crocodile.)
See item no. 309.

A Timorese myth and three fables.
See item no. 310.

Order in the Atoni house.
See item no. 327.

Splendid symbols: textiles and tradition in Indonesia.
See item no. 330.

Bunak

107 **Boiled woman and broiled man: myths and agricultural rituals of the Bunaq of central Timor.**
Claudine Friedberg.   In: *The flow of life: essays on eastern Indonesia.*
Edited by James J. Fox. Cambridge, Massachusetts: Harvard University Press, 1980, p. 266–89.

Friedberg outlines here some of the relationships between ritual power and political power in Bunak society, established by utilizing elements of the symbolic system at the level of social organization. Also dealt with is the problem of who holds the power to secure good harvests for the community through ritual practice.

108 **Cognation and generalized exchange: an Indonesian case study.**
David Hicks.   *Sociologus*, vol. 37, no. 2 (1987), p. 175–80. bibliog.

Over the last few years the author has been putting on record hitherto unknown relationship terminologies used by various peoples resident in eastern Indonesia, as well as establishing, by a series of original structural analyses, the respective characters of terminologies other fieldworkers have discovered. According to the author the Bunak are perhaps the only society in the world that combines a cognative terminology with a system of generalized exchange.

109 **Le savoir botanique des Bunaq: percevoir et classer dans le Haut Lamaknen (Timor, Indonésie).** (Botanical knowledge among the Bunak: perception and classification in Upper Lamaknen [Timor, Indonesia].)
Claudine Friedberg.   Paris: Editions du Muséum national d'Histoire naturelle, 1990. 155p. map. bibliog.

This detailed work represents the culmination of the author's research into Bunak botany and agriculture to date. By exposing what the Bunak know about plant morphology, growth and reproduction, she leads the reader to an insight into how the Bunak see the world and how they organize their society. There is a methodic inventory of Upper Lamaknen plants and an index of Bunak plant names.

110 **Ethnomédecine et ethnoscience: nosologie et etiologie chez les Bunaq de Timor (Indonésie).** (Ethnomedicine and ethnoscience: nosology and etiology among the Bunak of Timor, Indonesia.)
Claudine Friedberg. *Bulletin d'Ethnomédecine*, no. 24 (Oct. 1983), p. 37–57.

Discussed here is the Bunak concept of health and illness. After a short note on her research methodology, the author looks into their conception of a healthy body, the mythological origin of diseases, the causes of diseases, use of medicinal plants and practice of therapeutic techniques in daily life.

111 **La cuisine bunaq.** (Bunak food.)
Claudine Friedberg. *Asie du Sud-Est et Monde Insulindien*, vol. 9, no. 3–4 (1978), p. 215–27.

This article attempts to analyse the modes of cooking in terms of the requirements of the basic ingredients when cooked, the utensils and instruments used and the system of symbolic representation which a certain kind of preparation of ritual dishes imposes.

112 **La femme et le féminin chez les Bunaq du centre de Timor.** (The woman and the feminine among the Bunak of central Timor.)
Claudine Friedberg. *Archipel*, no. 13 (1977), p. 37–52.

Deals with the work allotted to women, primarily in the realm of agriculture, but also within the home.

113 **Repérage et découpage du temps chez les Bunaq du centre de Timor (avec deux contes traduits par L. Berthe).** (Estimation and subdivision of time among the Bunak of central Timor [with two tales translated by L. Berthe].)
Claudine Friedberg. *Archipel*, no. 6 (1973), p. 119–44.

The notion of time as it appears in the language and myths of the Bunak is analysed, especially with regard to the agricultural cycle. The author concludes that, in the absence of chronometers, the measurement of time is essentially subjective, but everyone needs to divide and count time to be able to order their existence.

114 **Socially significant plant species and their taxonomic positions among the Bunaq of central Timor.**
Claudine Friedberg. In: *Classifications and their social context.* Edited by Roy F. Ellen, David Reason. London: Academic Press, 1979, p. 81–101.

The work deals with the connection between the order which a population establishes in nature and the rest of the culture. The author focuses in particular on the folk classification of the Bunak, she selects a number of socially important plants and examines their classificatory position, but is not concerned with food plants or the general rôle of plants in myths. The plants which are socially the most important among the Bunak are the betel and the areca nut. The author discusses these and other plants as used ritually and considers the problem of ritual prohibition.

Agricultures timoraises. (Timorese agriculture.)
See item no. 287.

The development of traditional agricultural practices in Western Timor: from the ritual control of consumer goods production to the political control of prestige goods.
See item no. 288.

Social rituals of territorial management in light of Bunaq farming rituals.
See item no. 289.

Bei Gua, iténeraire de ancêtres: mythes des Bunaq de Timor. (Bei Gua, itinerary of ancestors: myths of the Bunak of Timor.)
See item no. 297.

Sur quelques distiques Buna' (Timor central). (Concerning some couplets of the Bunak [central Timor].)
See item no. 298.

Comment fut tranchée la liane celêste, et autre textes de littérature orale bunaq (Timor, Indonésie), recueillis et traduits par Louis Berthe. (How the heavenly liana was cut, and other oral literary texts of the Bunak [Timor, Indonesia] collected and translated by Louis Berthe.)
See item no. 304.

The weaving and waving of Nusa Tenggara Timur.
See item no. 333.

Cairui and Waimaka

115   **The Cairui and Uai Ma'a of Timor.**
David Hicks. *Anthropos*, vol. 68, no. 3–4 (1973), p. 473–81.
When the author collected the material for this brief ethnography these two groups were still quite remote from and less influenced by colonial life than other ethnic groups in Portuguese Timor.

Ema

116   **La cuisine ema.** (Ema food.)
Brigitte Clamagirand.   *Asie du Sud-Est et Monde Insulindien*, vol. 9,
no. 3–4 (1978), p. 199–213.
Describes the different courses of the meal, the kinds of food and their preparation.
The final part discusses cooking terminology. Boiled food is reserved for main meals, it
is associated with the house and belongs to the category of the cooked. Things grilled
are considered to be almost raw and are seen as snacks, in the same way as raw foods
such as fruit.

117   **The social organization of the Ema of Timor.**
Brigitte Clamagirand.   In: *The flow of life: essays on eastern Indonesia*.
Edited by James J. Fox. Cambridge, Massachusetts: Harvard
University Press, 1980, p. 134–51.
Clamagirand examines the main outlines of Ema society, concentrating on what
appears fundamental to the comprehension of the system of Ema social organization,
providing a general picture of the society.

118   **The relationship terminology of the Ema.**
David Hicks.   *Sociologus*, vol. 36, no. 2 (1986), p. 162–71. bibliog.
The system of affinity of the Ema belongs to the category generally described as
'asymmetric prescriptive alliance', a situation which is supported by analysis of the
Ema relationship terminology. The author points out, however, that some of the terms
indicate 'symmetric alliance'.

119   **Marobo: une société ema de Timor.** (Marobo: an Ema society in
Timor.)
Brigitte Renard-Clamagirand.   Paris: Centre de documentation et de
recherches sur l'Asie du sud-est et le monde insulindien, 1982. 490p.
map. bibliog. (Langues et Civilizations de l'Asie du Sud-Est et du
Monde Insulindien, no. 12).
By analysing the social organization and ritual practices of the Ema, the author
describes the relationship between the private and collective domains in their society,
revealing the basic unity of the social organization, ritual and myth. Social life
crystallizes around two poles: the lineage house and the community, defining two levels
of social organization.

Agricultures timoraises. (Timorese agriculture.)
See item no. 287.

**The development of traditional agricultural practices in Western Timor: from
the ritual control of consumer goods production to the political control of
prestige goods.**
See item no. 288.

La maison ema (Timor Portugais). (The house of the Ema [Portuguese Timor].)
See item no. 326.

Le travail du coton chez les Ema de Timor Portugais. (The use of cotton among the Ema of Portuguese Timor.)
See item no. 328.

Fatuluku

120 **Etudes sur les Fataluku (Timor Portugais) I: deux enquêtes à Timor Portugais chez les Fataluku de Lórehe.** (Studies on the Fataluku [Portuguese Timor] I: two enquiries in Portuguese Timor on the Fataluku of Lorehe.)
Maria Olímpia Lameiras Campagnolo. *Asie du Sud-Est et Monde Insulindien* vol. 3, no. 3, (Sept. 1972), p. 35–52. maps.
In the first part Maria Campagnolo gives a first evaluation of her two research missions among the Fataluku in 1966 and 1969–70. In the second part, Henri Campagnolo comments on a description of the Fataluku language and particularly the one spoken in Lorehe.

121 **Nári.**
F. Azevedo Gomes. *Geographica*, vol. 8, no. 31 (July 1972), p. 64–74. map.
Nári, a place of gigantic tombs, demolished dwellings, clearings once cultivated and worm-eaten sacred objects, on a rugged plateau in the centre of the Fataluku world is a place of great religious significance to the Fataluku.

Fataluku 1: relations et choix; introduction méthodologique à la description d'une langue 'non austronésienne' de Timor Oriental.
See item no. 154.

Rythmes et genres dans las littérature orale des Fataluku de Lorehe (Timor orientale), (Première partie). (Rhythms and genres in the literature of the Fataluku of Lorehe, East Timor. Part one.)
See item no. 299.

Makassai

122 **Descent, alliance and exchange ideology among the Makassae of East
Timor.**
Shepard Forman. In: *The flow of life: essays on eastern Indonesia.*
Edited by James J. Fox. Cambridge, Massachusetts: Harvard
University Press, 1980, p. 152–77.

Explores the cyclical relationship between marriage, birth and death and their related
rituals among the Makassai of East Timor, suggesting that exchange is the idiom of
their life, and that the continuity of alliance is deliberately marked and stressed in a
series of highly elaborated and specifically obligatory mortuary exchanges which far
outweigh more casual bridewealth negotiations in both their extent and their
significance.

123 **A transitional relationship terminology of assymetric prescriptive
alliance among the Makassai of eastern Indonesia.**
David Hicks. *Sociologus*, vol. 33, no. 1 (1983), p. 73–85. bibliog.

Rodney Needham, in various publications, has formulated a hypothetical model of the
development of relationship terminologies. This structural analysis of the Makassai
relationship terminology supplies empirical material which is consistent with Needham's model and shows a transitional stage in more detail.

**East Timor: exchange and political hierarchy at the time of the European
discoveries.**
See item no. 70.

Mambai

124 **O povo de Mambai: contribuição para o estudo do grupo linguístico
Mambai, Timor.** (The Mambai people: contributions to the study of the
Mambai linguistic group of Timor.)
António Duarte de Almeida e Carmo. *Estudos Políticos e Sociais*,
vol. 13, no. 14 (1965), p. 1233–368. maps. bibliog.

The Mambai live in the mountains and valleys of central East Timor, ranging from the
north to the south coast. They have a well-guarded system of beliefs and customs and
are often seen as the East Timorese ethnolinguistic group least affected by outside
influence. This is still the best general introduction to the Mambai of East Timor,
dealing at length with many aspects of Mambai life: their origins, history, geography,
family life, social life, food, arts and literature, religion, birth and childhood, marriage,
childbearing and death, and illustrated with photographs and sketches.

125 **Affines and the dead: Mambai rituals of alliance.**
Elizabeth G. Traube. *Bijdragen tot de Taal-, Land en Volkenkunde*, vol. 136, no. 1 (1980), p. 90–115.
The author relates how, among the Mambai, maritally related groups are required to cooperate in the disposal of the dead and how, underlying these death duties, is a concept of life as a balance between male and female.

126 **Cosmology and social life: ritual exchange among the Mambai of East Timor.**
Elizabeth G. Traube. Chicago: University of Chicago Press, 1986. 273p. bibliog.
The focus of this book is the ritual practices which the Mambai regard as central to their way of life. Reciprocity between life and death structures the Mambai ritual system, and all rituals are divided into categories of 'white', relating to agricultural fertility, and 'black' relating to the disposal of the dead. The Mambai carry on an intricate, richly textured, energetic ritual life with many performances drawn out over weeks or months.

127 **Mambai rituals of black and white.**
Elizabeth G. Traube. In: *The flow of life: essays on eastern Indonesia.* Edited by James J. Fox. Cambridge, Massachusetts: Harvard University Press, 1980, p. 290–314.
Investigates the language of Mambai religion and tries to communicate something of the atmosphere which surrounds religious utterances. The paper is organized around the complementary opposition of the two categories of ritual action, the 'white' and the 'black', but at the same time provides an outline of the total system by considering the set of ideas which underline all ritual performances.

Structural analysis in anthropology: case studies from Indonesia and Brazil. *See* item no. 144.

Uma lenda mambae. (A Mambai legend.) *See* item no. 312.

Rotinese and Ndaonese

128 **Between Savu and Roti: the transformation of social categories in the island of Ndao.**
James J. Fox. In: *A world of language: papers presented to Professor S.A. Wurm on his 65th birthday.* Edited by Donald C. Laycock, Werner Winter. Canberra: Research School of Pacific Studies, Australian National University, 1987, p. 195–203. bibliog. (Pacific Linguistics Series C, no. 100).

This is an analysis of the kinship terminology of Ndao, a small island some twelve kilometres to the west of Roti. The Ndaonese language is closely related to the language of Savu, which lies ninety kilometres to the west of Ndao, but for many years the island has been subject to cultural and political influence from Roti. This contact between Ndao and Roti is reflected in Ndaonese terminology of relationship which differs from what is found on either Savu or Roti. The author argues that an amalgamation of Rotinese and Savunese terms has transformed the Ndaonese terminology into a new system – one 'halfway' between Savu and Roti.

129 **Chicken bones and buffalo sinews: verbal frames and the organization of Rotinese mortuary performances.**
James J. Fox. In: *Time past, time present, time future: perspectives on Indonesia culture: essays in honour of P.E. de Josselin de Jong.* Edited by Henri J.M. Claessen, David S. Moyer. Dordrecht, The Netherlands; Providence, Rhode Island: Foris, 1988, p. 178–94 bibliog. (Verhandelingen van het Koninklijk Instituut voor Taal–, Land- en Volkenkunde, no. 131).

For the Rotinese, mortuary ceremonies are the most complex of their rituals. The performance of burial rites requires a minimum of three days and involves the attendance of hundreds of participants. In this paper the author considers the organization and sequencing of Rotinese mortuary practices in order to establish an understanding within which to examine Rotinese interpretations of their post-burial rituals, concluding that words, not performance, are the essence of the rites, providing continuation with the past, despite changes in performance.

130 **Island of gold- and silversmiths.**
James J. Fox. *Hemisphere*, vol. 22, no. 12 (Dec. 1978), p. 24–27. map.

This is a short introduction to the activities of the men of Ndao who are renowned throughout the region for the quality of their silversmithing skills. They traditionally spend the dry season travelling among the neighbouring islands, making jewellery on request. There are some colour photographs.

131 **Obligation and alliance: state structure and moiety organization in Thie, Roti.**
James J. Fox. In: *The flow of life: essays on eastern Indonesia.* Edited by James J. Fox. Cambridge, Massachusetts: Harvard University Press, 1980, p. 98–133.

Thie is one of the eighteen domains or *nusak* into which Roti is divided. This analyses the structure of the *nusak* and the rôle of marriage in the social and symbolic integration of the traditional state. The author provides an historical background to the Rotinese title system, outlining the basic opposition that underlies the titles. He examines their use in relation to the diversity of class and lineages within the *nusak* and focuses on marriage as the means of alliance and stratification among title-holding clans.

132 **Rotinese. Ndaonese.**
James J. Fox. In: *Ethnic groups of insular southeast Asia, vol. 1: Indonesia, Andaman Islands and Madagascar.* Edited by Frank M. LeBar. New Haven, Connecticut: Human Relations Area Files Press, 1972, p. 106–09. bibliog.

An introduction to the islands of Roti and Ndao, according to the standard LeBar formula.

133 **Sister's child as plant: metaphors in an idiom of consanguinity.**
James J. Fox. In: *Rethinking kinship and marriage.* Edited by Rodney Needham. London: Tavistock, 1971, . 219–52. bibliog.

Rotinese ritual and ordinary speech is suffused with highly involved botanical metaphors. Individuals, lineages and clans are said 'to plant' other individuals, lineages and clans and virtually the whole of Rotinese ritual life is concerned with caring for and making these 'plants' grow. In this detailed scholarly piece the author examines the relationship of the mother's brother to the sister's child.

134 **A tale of two states: ecology and the political economy of inequality on the island of Roti.**
James J. Fox. In: *Social and ecological systems.* Edited by P.C. Burnham, R.F. Ellen. London; New York; San Francisco: Academic Press, 1979, p. 19–42. map. bibliog.

Examines some of the material bases for social variation on Roti and considers the variation in historical perspective, Focusing on the *nusak* of Thie and Termanu, the author points out significant differences in their social and political organization, and considers how ecological, sociological and cultural variables have interacted in their divergent development. *Harvest of the palm* (q.v.) provides a background to this discussion.

135 **To the aroma of the name: the celebration of a Rotinese ritual of rock and tree.**
James J. Fox. *Bijdragen tot de Taal-, Land- en Volkenkunde*, vol. 145, no. 4 (1989), p. 520–38. bibliog.

This article describes the author's involvement in the initiation and performance of a ritual of *rock and tree* in honour of the Head of the Earth in the *nusak* of Termanu on Roti, based on the erection of a ring of raised stones around a large tree. The article examines Rotinese notions of ritual performance and the creation of ritual from poetic sources as well as the Rotinese concept of 'name'.

Rottineesch–Hollandsch woordenboek. (A Rotinese–Dutch dictionary.)
See item no. 157.

Rottineesch spraakkunst. (Rotinese grammar.)
See item no. 157.

The 'movement of the spirit' in the Timor area: Christian traditions and ethnic identities.
See item no. 172.

Adam and Eve on the island of Roti.
See item no. 300.

Our ancestors spoke in pairs: Rotinese views of language, dialect and code.
See item no. 301.

Retelling the past: the communicative structure of a Rotinese historical narrative.
See item no. 302.

To speak in pairs: essays on the ritual languages of eastern Indonesia.
See item no. 303.

Myths and legends of Indonesia.
See item no. 306.

Oral literature of Indonesia.
See item no. 314.

Splendid symbols: textiles and tradition in Indonesia.
See item no. 330.

Die primären Textiltechniken auf Sumba, Rote und Timor. (Primary methods of textile manufacture in Sumba, Roti and Timor.)
See item no. 332.

Sama-Bajau

136 **Notes on the southern voyages and settlements of the Sama-Bajau.**
James J. Fox. *Bijdragen tot de Taal-, Land- en Volkenkunde*, vol.
133, no. 4 (1977), p. 459–65.

This seafaring and fishing people originated in the Gulf of Bone in Sulawesi and are now scattered throughout the archipelago, including Nusa Tenggara Timur. They were probably voyaging to Timor as far back as the first quarter of the eighteenth century, and there are still small communities of them in Roti, Kupang Bay, and Ndao. These notes are based on published accounts of journeys in southeast Indonesia in the seventeenth and twentieth centuries and unpublished eighteenth-century records in the Algemeen Rijksarchief in The Hague.

The Sama-Bajau language in the Lesser Sunda Islands.
See item no. 165.

Eastern Tetun

137 **The Caraubalo Tetum.**
David Hicks. *Garcia de Orta, Série de Antropologia*, vol. 1, no. 1–2
(1973), p. 13–18. map.

David Hicks, the pre-eminent ethnographer of the eastern Tetun, outlines the descent, residence and affinal systems of this eastern Tetun group. The population of the village of Mamaluk is singled out for special attention and is shown to consist of two clans, one divided into five lineages, the other into three. Ideally, descent is patrilineal, residence is patrilocal and affinal arrangements are non-prescriptive.

138 **Conjonction féminine et disjonction masculine chez les Tetum (Timor,
Indonésie orientale).** (Feminine conjunction and masculine disjunction
among the Tetun [Timor, eastern Indonesia].)
David Hicks. *l'Homme*, vol. 25, no. 2 (April–June 1985), p. 23–36.
bibliog.

Argues that the Tetun impart responsibility to the male sex for what is termed the more 'disjunctive' foundations of social organization. By contrast, the women have control over the 'conjunctive' aspects of society and are responsible for the maintenance of life.

139 **Eastern Tetum.**
David Hicks. In: *Ethnic groups of insular southeast Asia, vol. 1: Indonesia, Andaman Islands and Madagascar.* Edited by Frank M. LeBar. New Haven, Connecticut: Human Relations Area Files Press, 1972, p. 98–103. bibliog.
A general introduction to the East Timorese, covering settlement pattern, housing, economy, kin groups, marriage and family, sociopolitical organization and religion.

140 **La compensation matrimoniale chez les Tetum.** (Tetun bridewealth.)
David Hicks. *l'Homme*, vol. 15, no. 3–4 (July–Dec. 1975), p. 55–65. bibliog.
This analysis shows how bridewealth acts as a selector for institutional possibilities among the Caraubalo Tetun. When bridewealth is given the mode of descent is patrilineal and the post-marital residence of the bridegroom is patrilocal. Strong links are forged between the bridegroom's relatives and those of his bride. If bridewealth is not given, the mode of descent is matrilineal, the bridegroom resides uxorilocally, and there are no links between the two families. The author maintains that, although lineal descent is an important Tetun institution, it is misleading to characterize the society as either patrilineal or matrilineal; a conclusion which may be far more typical of linear descent systems than many scholars may have supposed.

141 **Laver la jambe du buffle: un rite tetum.** (Washing the buffalo's leg: a Tetun ritual.)
David Hicks. *l'Homme*, vol. 14, no. 1 (Jan.–March 1974), p. 57–72. bibliog.
In this scholarly French-language article the author subjects the symbolism of the Caraubalo Tetun ritual known as 'washing the buffalo's leg' to structural analysis.

142 **Literary masks and metaphysical truths: intimations from Timor.**
David Hicks. *American Anthropologist*, vol. 90, no. 4 (Dec. 1988), p. 807–17. bibliog.
The author presents the argument that the oral literature of a non-literate society may provide a mode for transmitting ideas of a metaphysical nature. The main metaphysical idea transmitted in Tetun literature is that spirit and matter are a transformation of each other.

143 **A maternal religion: the rôle of women in Tetum myth and ritual.**
David Hicks. De Kalb, Illinois: Northern Illinois University, Center for Southeast Asian Studies, 1984. 141p. map. bibliog. (Monograph Series on Southeast Asia, Special Report, no. 22).
This describes various ritual and mythological ways in which women dominate men among the Tetun, especially in religious life.

144 **Structural analysis in anthropology: case studies from Indonesia and Brazil.**
David Hicks. St. Augustin bei Bonn, Germany: Verlag des Anthropos-Instituts, 1978. 133p. bibliog. (Studia Instituti Anthropos, no. 30).

In ten essays the author uses the concepts of structural analysis and the methodological tools it exploits to resolve certain empirical problems raised by ethnographic data from Brazil and eastern Indonesia. The Indonesian data has been included in six chapters on literary and ritual symbols, classification, bridewealth, institutional possibilities and relationship terminology among the Tetun and asymmetric prescriptive alliance among the Mambai.

145 **Tetum descent.**
David Hicks. *Anthropos*, vol. 82, no. 1–3 (1987). p. 47–61. bibliog.

In this brief outline, the author describes the institution of descent among the Tetun as being defined by a combination of the different options available to them when marriages are contracted, consideration of bridewealth combined with variations in post-marital residence.

146 **Tetum ghosts and kin; fieldwork in an Indonesian community.**
David Hicks. Palo Alto, California: Mayfield, 1976. 143p. map. bibliog.; Prospect Heights, Illinois: Waveland, 1988, 2nd ed. (Exploration in World Ethnology Series.)

Written in a plain, non-academic style, with accompanying photographs and glossaries of Tetun and anthropological terms, this is an excellent introduction to Tetun kinship and kinship in general. The chief academic purpose of the book is to show how ritual in a non-literate community brings together many facets of that community's culture – religious beliefs, kinship practices, literature, ecology, the architecture of the house and unites them in a comprehensive system. An Indonesian-language version also appeared under the title *Roh orang Tetum di Timor Timur* (Jakarta: Penerbit Sinar Harapan, 1985).

Tetun–English dictionary.
See item no. 160.

The formation of Tetun-Praça, vehicular language of East Timor.
See item no. 163.

Space, motion and symbol in Tetum religion
See item no. 167.

The Tetum folktale as a sociological, cosmological and logical model (Timor).
See item no. 305.

Timor: legends and poems from the land of the sleeping crocodile. Book 1.
See item no. 311.

Art and religion on Timor.
See item no. 321.

Western Tetun

147 **Northern Belunese (Timor) marriage and kinship: a study of symbols.**
Ernest Brandewie, Simon Asten. *Philippine Quarterly of Culture and Society*, vol. 4, no. 1 (March 1976), p. 19–30. bibliog.
In this brief report, some of the symbols surrounding marriage among the Northern Tetun are presented. In doing so, many of the major concerns of the Tetun, their way of conceiving of marriage, the dualistic character of their outlook and the logic of their symbol-set are expressed.

148 **Incursions upon Wehali: a modern history of an ancient empire.**
Gérard Francillon. In: *The flow of life: essays on eastern Indonesia.*
Edited by James J. Fox. Cambridge, Massachusetts: Harvard University Press, 1980, p. 248–65.
At the time of research Wehali was a small princedom in the southern portion of the *kabupaten* of Belu in central Timor, the most fertile part of the island. The author gives an unadorned history of traditional and colonial administration for the period until 1974, of this most isolated of Tetun-speaking communities.

149 **Un profitable échange de frères chez les Tetun du Sud, Timor central.**
(A profitable exchange of brothers among the Southern Tetun, central Timor.)
Gérard Francillon. *l'Homme*, vol. 29, no. 1 (1989), p. 26–43. bibliog.
The southern coastal Tetun of central Timor have a double system of matrilineal succession and of uxorilocal residence. This system and the strongly feminist ideology and practice mean that brothers, not sisters, are exchanged at marriage.

150 **Confirmations and corrections: Tetum terms of relationship from central Timor.**
David Hicks. *Sociologus*, vol. 39, no. 2 (1989), p. 152–60.
In this scholarly piece Hicks compares some kinship terminology from his 1981 article in *Sociologus*, ('A two-section system with matrilineal descent among the Tetun of eastern Indonesia', see item no. 151), with some terms collected by Vroklage, published in his *Ethnographie der Belu* (q.v.).

151 **A two-section system with matrilineal descent among the Tetun of eastern Indonesia.**
David Hicks. *Sociologus*, vol. 31, no. 2 (1981), p. 180–84. bibliog.
This short article takes the results of Brandewie and Asten's work (q.v.) and orders it into a format conventionally followed in the analysis of relationship terms. Although important from an anthropological angle as it describes the first matrilineal two-section system ever discovered in Indonesia, unfortunately it is only for those familiar with the anthropological context.

152 **Emerging hierarchies: processes of stratification and early state formation in the Indonesian archipelago: prehistory and the ethnographic present.**
Ina. E. Slamet-Velsink. PhD thesis, Leiden University, 1986. map. bibliog.

A clearly written introduction to the Western Tetun, their economy, kinship and social stratification, contrasting the Northern Tetun, who live in the mountains of the central and north part of West Timor, with the Southern Tetun who inhabit the densely populated coastal plain of the south coast – the old kingdom of Wehali.

153 **Ethnographie der Belu in Zentral-Timor.** (The ethnography of the Belu in central Timor.)
Bernardus Andreas Gregorius Vroklage. Leiden, The Netherlands: E.J. Brill, 1952. 3 vols.

Despite its age this book remains a classic of ethnography of a Timorese people. The first two volumes offer a daunting prospect of more than 900 pages of unrelieved text, dealing with every aspect of Northern and Southern Tetun life from their environment to their kinship structure. The third volume is a folio of 426 photographs relevant to the text – textiles, dignitaries, basketware, pottery, hunting, daily life, games, tattoos, cockfighting, buildings. The quantity, quality and scope of these photographs make them an important document in themselves.

Tetun–English dictionary.
See item no. 160.

Agricultures timoraises. (Timorese agriculture.)
See item no. 287.

The development of traditional agricultural practices in western Timor: from the ritual control of consumer goods production to the political control of prestige goods.
See item no. 288.

Sociological interpretation of differences in musical styles of the southern Tetun (Timor).
See item no. 320.

Languages

154 **Fataluku 1: relations et choix; introduction méthodologique à la description d'une langue 'non austronésienne' de Timor Oriental.**
(Fataluku 1: relations and choice; a methodological introduction to the description of a 'non-Austronesian' language of East Timor.)
Henri Campagnolo.   Paris: Centre national de la recherche scientifique, société d'études linguistiques et anthropologiques de France, centre de documentation et de recherche sur l'Asie du sud-est et le monde insulindien, 1979. 246p. map. bibliog. (Langues et Civilisations de l'Asie du Sud-Est et du Monde Insulindien, no. 5).
This is an essay in general linguistics which draws upon the study of the Fataluku language. A brief introductory chapter, written in collaboration with Maria-Olimpia Lameiras Campagnolo, situates the language community geographically and ethnologically, and provides a brief description of the linguistic field work and its relationship to the ethnological work. The remainder of the volume is concerned with the theoretical questions posed by the Fataluku language.

155 **An Indonesian-English dictionary.**
John M. Echols, Hassan Shadily, revised and edited by John U. Wolff, James T. Collins in cooperation with Hassan Shadily.   Ithaca, New York; London: Cornell University Press, 1989. 3rd ed. 618p.
Indonesian is widely used through both West and East Timor in administration and education. This is still very much the standard dictionary for students of the Indonesian language. Revised and expanded, this new edition retains the two features which make it such a useful dictionary. Firstly, the specific meaning of each entry is defined by the use of illuminatory example phrases and secondly the open *e* sound is denoted by *é*.

49

156 **Kamus Inggris–Indonesia.** (An English–Indonesian dictionary.)
John M. Echols, Hassan Shadily.   Ithaca, New York; London: Cornell
University Press; Jakarta: P.T. Gramedia, 1975. 660p.

Prepared primarily for the use of Indonesians, but useful for speakers of English who wish to find the Indonesian equivalent for an English word or phrase. Orthography and pronunciation guides are according to American usage.

157 **Rottineesch–Hollandsch woordenboek.** (A Rottinese–Dutch dictionary.)
J.C.G. Jonker.   Leiden, The Netherlands: E.J. Brill, 1908. 806p.

This, along with the same author's treatise on the Rotinese language, *Rottineesch spraakkunst* (Leiden, The Netherlands: E.J. Brill, 1915. 714p.) are the most complete Western-language descriptions.

158 **Standard Indonesian made simple.**
Liaw Yock Fang, with the assistance of Nini Tiley-Notodisuryo.
Singapore, Kuala Lumpur: Times Books International, 1990. 440p.

This is an intensive language course designed to take three months. There are twenty lessons, each one covering conversation, sentence patterns, grammar, word formation and numerous exercises. There is also a section of selected readings from newspapers, magazines and books, introducing useful, up-to-date vocabulary.

159 **Proeve van een Timorese grammatica.** (An interim Timorese grammar.)
Pieter Middelkoop.   *Bijdragen tot de Taal-, Land- en Volkenkunde*,
vol. 106 (1957), p. 375–517.

Until the ascendancy of Indonesian as the national language in the post-war years, Atoni was the language of the upland areas of West Timor, and is still widely spoken, often referred to as Dawan. This Dutch-language study is primarily a technical grammar aimed at linguistics specialists rather than the student, but it is, however, a lucid and comprehensive introduction, covering pronunciation, morphology and syntax.

160 **Tetun–English dictionary.**
Cliff Morris.   Canberra: Australian National University, Department
of Linguistics, Research School of Pacific Studies, 1984. 194p. (Pacific
Linguistics Series C, no. 83).

Tetun has for centuries been an historically influential language throughout the island of Timor. It is presently spoken in varying degrees of expertise and in a number of regional dialects. As a soldier in East Timor during the Second World War the author learned Tetun-Los, and it is that dialect of Tetun which forms the basis of this dictionary. Emphasis has been given to the explanation of words involving the ritual practices of birth, marriage, death, food growing and religion. There is a useful section on grammar and syntax, specific to Tetun-Los, but other dialects have not been neglected, and words peculiar to other dialects and particular places have been recorded as such.

161 **A contemporary Indonesian–English dictionary.**
A.E. Schmidgall-Tellings, Alan M. Stevens. Chicago; Athens, Ohio;
London: Ohio University Press, 1981. 388p.

Complementary in style to the dictionaries of Echols and Shadily (q.v.), this is a supplement to the standard Indonesian dictionaries with particular concentration on new words, expressions and meanings. An Indonesian edition was produced in Medan, published by Toko Buku Deli in 1982.

162 **Holle lists: vocabularies in languages of Indonesia. Vol. 6: Lesser Sunda Islands.**
W.A.L. Stockhof, in cooperation with Lia Saleh-Bronkhorst, Alma E.
Almanar. Canberra: Research School of Pacific Studies, Australian
National University, 1983. 337p. map. (Series D, no. 59; Materials in
Languages of Indonesia no. 22).

In 1880 K.F. Holle (1829–96) proposed to prepare a short list of approximately 1,000 lexical items for dispersion throughout the Dutch colony in order to obtain a more detailed knowledge of the linguistic situation of the archipelago. The 234 lists remaining in the National Museum in Jakarta contain materials on quite a number of languages and dialects which are not well-known or have even never been studied. The lists would be of particular use to those conducting comparative and descriptive work. Lists of relevance to Timor are List 18a Termanu (Roti), p. 19; List 18b Ba'a (Roti), p. 37; List 52 Belu/Tetun, p. 59; List 90 Belu/Tetun, p. 71; List 116 Belu/Tetun (Central Timor), p. 87; List 127 Marae (Central Timor), p. 101. These lists should be used in conjunction with vol. 1 (Series D, no. 17), 1980, which contains the introduction, the masterlist and the indexes.

163 **The formation of Tetun-Praça, vehicular language of East Timor.**
Luís Filipe F.R. Thomaz. In: *Papers on Indonesian languages and
literature*. Edited by Nigel Phillips, Khaidir Anwar. London, Paris:
Cahìers d'Archipel, 1981, p. 54–79. maps. bibliog.

The author discusses the history of Tetun-Praça, a simplified Portuguese-influenced version of Tetun which developed in Dili, how it became the *lingua franca* before the arrival of the Portuguese, loan words and the loan of grammatical constructions. He then shows the adaptation of the language to new needs and conditions and illustrates the interdependence between linguistic and historical evolution, using examples from eight texts ranging from classical Tetun to the political language of Fretilin.

164 **Language atlas of the Pacific area.**
Edited by Stephen A. Wurm, Shirô Hattori, cartography by Theo
Baumann. Canberra: The Australian Academy of the Humanities in
collaboration with the Japan Academy, 1981. bibliog.

Part 2, sheet 40, 'Lesser Sunda Islands and Timor' is a clearly presented, colour map showing the geographical distribution of the languages spoken in Timor and Roti, with an indication of the numbers of speakers of each languages and many other notes.

Languages

165 **The Sama–Bajau language in the Lesser Sunda Islands.**
Jilis A.J. Verheijen.   Canberra: Australian National University,
Research School of Pacific Studies, 1986. 209p. map. bibliog. (Pacific
Linguistics Series D, no. 70; Materials in Languages of Indonesia, no.
32).

The Sama–Bajau have villages throughout the archipelago including the villages of
Sulamu near Kupang and Oé Nggaé on Roti. Besides a description and discussion of
the language, dictionaries and some literary texts, there is also relevant information on
general Sama–Bajau history.

Timor, quatro séculos de colonização portuguesa. (Timor: four centuries of
Portuguese colonization.)
See item no. 74.

The people and languages of Timor.
See item no. 93.

Our ancestors spoke in pairs: Rotinese views of language, dialect and code.
See item no. 301.

To speak in pairs: essays on the ritual languages of eastern Indonesia.
See item no. 303.

Religion

Traditional Timorese

166 **Southeast Asian religions: insular cultures.**
James J. Fox. In: *Encyclopedia of religion*. Edited by Mircea Eliade.
New York: Macmillan; London: Collier Macmillan, 1986, vol. 13,
p. 520–30. map. bibliog.
An excellent introduction to the main features that indigenous insular southeast Asian religions have in common – the prevalence of complementary duality, the belief in the immanence of life and in the interdependence of life and death, the reliance on specific rituals to mark stages in the processes of life and death, the celebration of spiritual differentiation. All these notions are regarded here as part of a commmon Austronesian conceptual heritage.

167 **Space, motion and symbol in Tetum religion.**
David Hicks. In: *Indonesian religions in transition*. Edited by Rita
Smith Kipp, Susan Rodgers. Tucson, Arizona: University of Arizona
Press, 1987, p. 35–47. map.
This is an investigation into how religion can find accommodation with notions of space in story-telling, analysing two narratives and relating their form and contents to the religion of the people who tell them, the Tetun.

168 **Curse, retribution, enmity as data in natural religion, especially in Timor, confronted with scripture.**
Pieter Middlekoop. Amsterdam: Jacob van Campen, 1960. 168p.
bibliog.
Middlekoop's works, pre-eminent in the study of the Atoni people, are seldom accompanied by any introductory or explanatory notes, making them opaque and difficult for those not familiar with his context. As a priest in West Timor he noticed the importance of curse, retribution and enmity to the local population and here

discusses the way curses and retribution are dealt with in the Bible and their translation into Atoni.

East of Bali: from Lombok to Timor.
See item no. 9.

To the aroma of the name: the celebration of a Rotinese ritual of rock and tree.
See item no. 135.

A maternal religion: the rôle of women in Tetum myth and ritual.
See item no. 143.

Christianity

169   **Adat and christianity in Nusa Tenggara Timur: reaction and countereaction.**
Rex Alexander Francis Paul Webb.   *Philippine Quarterly of Culture and Society*, vol. 14, no. 4 (Dec. 1986), p. 339–65.
A discussion of the problems encountered when Christian missionaries come into close contact with traditonal ethics, morality and cultural and religious beliefs. The dichotomy between what the Christian missionary sees as the 'better' way and the old tried and tested ways of the indigenous inhabitants is something which cannot be easily solved.

170   **East Timor: a christian reflection. Timor Oriental: une reflexion chrétienne.**
Catholic Institute for International Relations.   London: Catholic Institute for International Relations, 1987. 21p.
The Catholic church has always been one of the major forces in East Timorese society. This short pamphlet, in English and French, admits with a sense of remorse that 'in the past our churches have forsaken their true responsibilities. This was especially true during the period when our countries were colonizing powers'. The church is now trying to focus outside attention on the situation in the territory and on the struggle against annexation and human rights atrocities.

171   **Revival in Timor.**
Frank L. Cooley.   *Southeast Asia Journal of Theology*, vol. 14, no. 2 (1973), p. 78–94.
The author's personal impression of the revival, which began in September 1965 in the mountains of central Timor, is that for the actual team members it has meant a deepening of their faith and a fuller maturity of Christian life. He concludes that the movement did have, at least for a time and in some areas, a visibly positive influence on society.

172 **The 'movement of the spirit' in the Timor area: Christian traditions and ethnic identities.**
James J. Fox. In: *Indonesia: Australian perspectives. Indonesia: the making of a culture*. Edited by James J. Fox. Canberra: Australian National University Research School of Pacific Studies, 1980, p. 235–46. map. bibliog.
Excellent, almost day-by-day account, of the revival and its impact in Roti. The wariness of the Rotinese was in contrast to the Timorese who were much more willing to accept it. In light of this, the author describes the distinct styles of religious experience that distinguish different ethnic groups of the region.

173 **The Franciscans on the island of Timor.**
Achilles Meersman. In: *The Franciscans in the Indonesian archipelago, 1300–1775*. Louvain, Belgium: Nauwelaerts, 1967, p. 145–54. map. bibliog.
Based on necrologies of Franciscan friars who died in Portuguese Timor, this is a rather sketchy article, giving no idea of the organization of the missions and their methods or the effect of their actions on the indigenous population.

174 **Indonesian revival: focus on Timor.**
George W. Peters. Grand Rapids, Michigan: Zondervan Publishing House, 1974. 117p. map. bibliog.
The author made a personal journey to Timor to evaluate the effects of the revival, revealing his findings in this small-format paperback in a laboured, anecdotal style. He was rather dismayed to find that it had lost its intial fire and zeal, but is hopeful that 'the Holy Spirit will become evident again burning away much of the dross, the demonic . . . and the fleshy'.

175 **Die katholische Missionschule in Nusa Tenggara Timur (Süd Ost Indonesien) ihre geschichtliche Entfaltung und ihre Bedeutung für die Missionsarbeit.** (The history of the development of the Catholic missionschools in Nusa Tenggara Timur [southeast Indonesia] and their impact on missionary work.)
P. Kurt Piskaty. Aachen, Germany: Steyler Verlag, 1964. map. bibliog. (Studia Instituti Missiologici Societas Verbi Divini, no. 5).
A well-documented study of schools in Flores and Timor between 1913 and 1963, focusing on the educational activities of the Societas Verbi Divini missionary society, but bringing in wider concepts of development and education.

176 **The church and the sandalwood islands: protestants and catholics in Sumba and Timor, 1960–1980.**
Rex Alexander Francis Paul Webb. Townsville, Australia: James Cook University of North Queenland, 1980. 29p. map. bibliog. (Southeast Asian Studies Committee Occasional Paper, no. 4).
A survey of the positions and exploits of various Protestant and Catholic denomination churches in Sumba and West Timor. The Indonesian coup of 1965 had a strong influence on the number of converts to the churches. Special attention is given to the revival and the churches' considerable rôle in education, agriculture and public health. Much of the material in this monograph is also discussed in detail in *Palms and the cross* (q.v.), but this version is brief and to the point.

177 **Old lamps for new: recent developments in Nusa Tenggara Timur.**
Rex Alexander Francis Paul Webb. *Sojourn*, vol. 4, no. 2 (Aug. 1989), p. 205–32. bibliog.
Since the 1950s, the Catholic and Protestant churches have tried to improve socio-economic conditions in Nusa Tenggara Timur, initiating many small-scale labour-intensive and reasonably successful development projects and expanding educational facilities. Lately, the government has joined churches with several prestigious capital-intensive, high-technology projects. The author's overview of many projects shows that local leaders, fearing a loss of power and authority, sometimes oppose projects to the detriment of the local population. Proper consultation and the availability of local knowledge are instrumental in keeping projects from floundering.

178 **Palms and the cross: socio-economic development in Nusatenggara, 1930–1975.**
Rex Alexander Francis Paul Webb. Townsville, Australia: James Cook University of North Queenland, 1986. 284p. maps. bibliog. (Centre for Southeast Asian Studies Monograph, no. 15.)
During the period under discussion Indonesia suffered four traumatic events which affected both nation and churches: the depression of the 1930s, the Japanese occupation, independence, and the events of 1965. They all made a significant impact on life in the region, and the effects were rather unique in this predominately Christian part of the country. In plotting these effects, the author has produced the major English-language work on the church in Timor, which is detailed, well-researched and written, and both analytical and critical.

179 **The people of the book: christians and muslims in Indonesia: a brief survey of Nusa Tenggara Timur.**
Rex Alexander Francis Paul Webb. *Indonesia Circle*, no. 35 (Nov. 1984), p. 56–69. bibliog.
There is a short historical survey of the coming of Islam and Christianity to Indonesia and Nusa Tenggara Timur. Attention is given to development aid, Christian institutes, Pancasila the Indonesian state ideology which stresses the worship of only one God, the aftermath of the coup in 1965 and the rôle of the Department of Religion.

180   **The sickle and the cross: christians and communists in Bali, Flores,
       Sumba and Timor, 1965–67.**
       Rex Alexander Francis Paul Webb. *Journal of Southeast Asian
       Studies*, vol. 17, no. 1 (March 1986), p. 94–112.
Communist Party influence in Nusa Tenggara Timur was slight in comparison with
Java, Sumatra and Bali, but the general desperate economic plight of the region made
the Communists' promise of better economic conditions and land reform quite
attractive. The author discusses the acts of individual courage undertaken by Catholics
and Protestants on behalf of victims during the anti-Communist backlash following the
events of September 1965, and contrasts them with the timidity of the institutionalized
hierarchy of the Catholic and Protestant churches.

A ordem de São Domingos e as origens de Timor. (The Dominican Order and
the origins of Timor.)
See item no. 67

**Curse, retribution, enmity as data in natural religion, especially in Timor,
confronted with scripture.**
See item no. 168.

Adat and christianity in Nusa Tenggara Timur: reaction and counterreaction.
See item no. 169.

Adam and Eve on the island of Roti.
See item no. 300.

Social Conditions

181 **I am Timorese: testimonies from East Timor.**
Catholic Institute for International Relations. London: Catholic
Institute for International Relations, 1990. 39p.
Testimonies can never truly reflect the experience of all of Timor's people. Of the ten
people who speak in this collection, few are from the countryside where conditions are
most harsh, few women are represented and those who have spoken have been able to
leave East Timor, are relatively well-educated and have spent much time of the
occupation living in Dili. But testimonies have become a vital source of information on
conditions in East Timor during a period of very limited access for independent
observers.

182 **East Timor after integration.**
Department of Foreign Affairs. Jakarta: Republic of Indonesia,
Department of Foreign Affairs, 1984. 2nd ed. 143p.
'Joined by Indonesian volunteers who had responded to the call of their Timorese
brothers for aid, the forces of the four (political) parties pressed speedily forward and
captured Dili on December 7, 1975. The liberation of Dili ended 4 months of
bloodshed and suffering for the East Timorese'. This glossy, full-colour production
presents Indonesia's reasoned version of their invasion of East Timor to overseas
readers.

183 **Feto Rai Timor. Mulheres de Timor.** (Women of Timor.)
Fundação de Relações Internacionais; Em Timor-Leste, A Paz é
Possivél; Commissão para os direitos do Povo Maubere; Pascoela
Barreto. Lisbon: The Authors, 1991. 33p. map.
Timorese women give testimonies of their experiences in East Timor and as refugees
abroad.

184 **Indonesia's newest minority: the East Timorese.**
Helen Mary Hill. In : *World Minorities 1*. Edited by Georgina
Ashworth. Sunbury, England: Quartermaine House & Minority Rights
Group, 1977, p. 89–93. bibliog.
A very brief descriptive treatise on the history of East Timor, the events of 1974 and
1975 and social conditions at the time of writing.

185 **Indonesia's annexation of East Timor: political, administrative and
developmental initiatives.**
J. Stephen Hoadley. In: *Southeast Asian Affairs 1977*. Singapore:
Heinemann Educational Books, 1977, p. 133–42.
One year after integration the author describes early Indonesian–Timorese links,
Indonesia's interest in bringing East Timor under Indonesian influence, Indonesia's
Timor strategy, the civil war between Fretilin (Frente Revolucionaria de Timor Leste
Independente) and the UDT (União Democrática Timorense) and Indonesian inter-
vention. He also discusses the provisional territorial assembly, legal instruments of
integration, financing and administering East Timor and development priorities.

186 **East Timor.**
Indonesia Reports, no. 53 (March 1991), 39p.
Translation of chapters 2, 3, 4, part of chapter 5 and chapter 6 of the Universitas
Gadjah Mada's Center for the Study of Rural and Regional Devlopment's (P3PK) final
report on an investigation it conducted in East Timor in late 1989 and early 1990. The
study appeared in 1990 as *A socio-anthropological study of East Timorese society*. It is
probably the most candid assessment of some major problems in East Timor ever
ventured by Indonesian researchers. The perspective is distinctly pro-Indonesian
integrationist, but it contains much useful information. The Research Team Chairman
was Prof. Dr. Mubyarto, senior researcher Dr. Loekman Soetrisno, and assistant
researchers Drs. Hudiyanto, Drs. Edhie Djatmiko, Dra. Ita Setiawati and Dra. Agnes
Mawarni. Major subjects are: theoretical framework and methodology, role of the
church, local government and army; case studies in Ainaro and Ermera districts on
environmental and social conditions and social, political and religious structures.

187 **Dili: panorama de uma sociedade.** (Dili: panorama of a society.)
Carlos M.G. Ramos de Oliveira. *Boletim de Sociedade de Geografia
de Lisboa*, vol. 89, nos. 1–3 (Jan.–March 1971), p. 33–49.
Colonial Dili was a primarily commercial and administrative centre with four distinct
ethno-cultural groups: Europeans, Chinese, Timorese and Arabs. Each lived in their
own area of town, each group distributing itself according to groups, always reflecting a
certain level of education. The hierarchy of social strata closely followed the distinction
between the ethnic cultural groups. The not very dynamic economy did not stimulate
greater social mobility.

188 **Pasar dan integrasi di Timor Timur.** (The market and national
integration in East Timor.)
Abdul Rachman Patji. *Masyarakat Indonesia*, vol. 14, no. 3 (Dec.
1987), p. 269–94. bibliog.
The article describes market developments in East Timor and what this development
has contributed to the process of integrating East Timor into the Republic of
Indonesia. According to the author, in terms of economic structure, the market in East
Timor has increased new economic activity among the indigenous population. In terms
of public institutions, it has minimized differentiation in the structure of society. The
market has become a medium for social and cultural interaction between the
indigenous people and migrants from other Indonesian provinces.

189 **East Timor: beyond hunger: analysis of famine, 1979–1980.**
Southeast Asia Chronicle, no. 74. (Aug. 1980). 28p. map.
A special edition on East Timor, with articles by Noam Chomsky on US government
and American news media rôles, on Fretilin and its continued resistance despite
serious setbacks, on relief efforts, and an article by Rear Admiral Gene R. La Rocque
claiming that Indonesia is only of limited military importance to the United States –
certainly not enough to justify United States support for the invasion of East Timor.
Finally, there are translations into English of four poems by the revolutionary
Timorese poet Francisco Borja da Costa, killed by invading Indonesian paratroopers in
December 1975.

190 **The Indonesianization of East Timor.**
Donald E. Weatherbee. *Contemporary Southeast Asia*, vol. 3, no. 1
(June 1981), p. 1–23.
The author visited East Timor in late May and early June 1980, and this covers internal
and external developments affecting East Timor up until that time: the casualties of the
struggle, the weaknesses of Fretilin and the economic and administrative integration of
East Timor into Indonesia. Beginning with the premise that the Indonesian annexation
is irreversible he discusses how Indonesia had fitted East Timor into the country's
administrative framework and how it had set about developing the territory
economically. The background and conditions of the author's visit to East Timor are
given in his article: *The situation in East Timor* (Institute of International Studies,
University of South Carolina, 1980. [Occasional Paper, no. 1]).

'Opening up': travellers' impressions of East Timor, 1989–1991.
See item no. 29.

East Timor: a christian reflection. Timor Oriental: une reflexion chrétienne.
See item no. 170

Old lamps for new: recent developments in Nusa Tenggara Timur.
See item no. 177.

Palms and the cross: socio-economic development in Nusatenggara, 1930–1975.
See item no. 178.

East Timor today.
See item no. 276.

Indonesian Invasion
and Foreign Relations

General

191 **The war against East Timor.**
Carmel Budiarjo, Liem Soei Liong.   London: Zed, Marran;
Haarlem, The Netherlands: In de Knipscheer; Leichhardt, Australia:
Pluto, 1984. 248p. maps. bibliog.
Two-thirds of this book is original text, the rest being a translation of nine secret
Indonesian army documents captured in December 1982. It is particularly strong on
the structure and organization of the Indonesian military, their operations in East
Timor and the Timorese resistance. It also gathers together much information
previously only available in leaflets, bulletins, newsletters and a wide range of other
sources from Fretilin reports to CIA intelligence reports and interviews with Timorese
churchmen. The work is marred by a generally uncritical presentation of Fretilin.

192 **Timor: um grito.** (Timor: a cry.)
Jorge Barros Duarte.   Lisbon: Pentaedro, 1988. 129p.
The author was born in Same in East Timor, trained in theology in Macau and in 1965
was elected to represent Timor at the National Assembly in Lisbon. He has produced
various works on a variety of Timorese subjects.

193 **Timor: a people betrayed.**
James Stanley Dunn. Milton, Australia: Jacaranda Press, 1983. 384p.
3 maps.

A good introduction, explaining how events unfolded leading up to the abortive decolonization of East Timor and the tragedy which followed. The author, an Australian consul in East Timor during the 1960s, sets out to answer a number of questions concerning the nature of the Portuguese and Indonesian presences in the territory, the nature of Fretilin and the apparent failure of Australia to respond to the situation. For the years following the invasion the author has relied on interviews with Timorese refugees and leaders of Timorese political parties, the study of messages sent via Darwin from Fretilin and information from Indonesian sources.

194 **Timor and West Irian: the reasons why.**
Peter Hastings. In: *Indonesia: the making of a nation.* Edited by
J.A.C. Mackie. Canberra: Research School of Pacific Studies,
Australian National University, 1980, p. 713–18.

The author argues, clearly and lucidly, against the 'expansionist Indonesia' school of thought on East Timor, claiming the major element in Jakarta's decision to annex East Timor was the uncertainty attending any change in sovereignty once Portugal had abdicated all political responsibility for its former colony. In terms of justification he compares it with the Dutch-Australian invasion of East Timor in the Second World War.

195 **Timor: past and present.**
Finngeir Hiorth. Townsville, Australia: James Cook University of
North Queensland, 1985. 98p. map. bibliog. (Southeast Asian
monographs, no. 17).

Although mainly devoted to the political background of the developments in East Timor there is more attention to the geographical, economic, social, prehistoric and linguistic background than in most comparable accounts. There are also more facts relating to West Timor, showing that integration may have its advantages as well as disadvantages, serving to unite a divided island with much in common by way of heritage.

196 **East Timor; nationalism and colonialism.**
Jill Jolliffe. St. Lucia, Australia: University of Queensland Press,
1978. 304p. maps.

The author served as a journalist in East Timor during the civil war between Fretilin and UDT until directly before the invasion and offers little analysis or commentary on the events she describes, preferring to recount them in a clear journalistic style. Assuming that Fretilin would have played a major part in any independent East Timorese government, this is, in fact, largely a history of the development of Fretilin. An abridged and updated version of this work appeared as *Timor: terra sangrenta.* (Timor: bloodied land), (Lisbon: O Jornal, 1989. 172p. map. bibliog.). It looks more closely at the Portuguese colonial record and includes some testimonies of those affected by the situation.

197 An act of genocide: Indonesia's invasion of East Timor.
Arnold Kohen, John Taylor. London: TAPOL, 1979. 133p. maps.
A detailed, carefully documented pro-Fretilin account of four aspects of the conflict in
East Timor. Firstly there is a general account of the history of the conflict up until
1979. There is then an account of Indonesian atrocities alleged to have been committed
during the conflict, an account of the complicity and acquiesence of the United States,
Australia, Portugal, the United Kingdom, the Netherlands and a chapter on the rights
of the East Timorese to determine their own political future.

198 Patterns of conflict in eastern Indonesia.
Justus M. van der Kroef. *Conflict Studies*, no. 79 (Jan. 1977), 16p.
map.
The author explains the background to resistance movements in Irian Jaya, where
there was a controversial takeover of the Netherlands East Indies possession, and East
Timor. The article covers events concerning the takeover and discusses them in the
context of Indonesia's security policy, and the way these policies are tied into the
economic needs of the country.

199 The historical roots of Indonesian irredentism.
Kwa Chong Guan. *Asian Studies*, vol. 8, no. 1 (April 1970), p. 38–52.
The author discusses Indonesia's historical claims and rights over surrounding
territories, including East Timor, in the interests of the creation of a Pan-Indonesian
nation.

200 Indonesia and the incorporation of East Timor.
Michael Leifer. *The World Today*, vol. 32, no. 9 (Sept. 1976),
p. 347–54.
This examines the motivation and character of Indonesia's intervention in, and
subsequent annexation of, Portuguese Timor. It argues that the 'rudimentary' politics
of the eastern half of the island followed a course which served Indonesian interests,
especially in providing a justification for intervention that was absent at the outset.
Although this appears to be rather drily academic at first, at the close it can be seen to
be a rather subtle critique of Indonesia's actions.

201 Indonesia's foreign policy.
Michael Leifer. London: George Allen & Unwin, 1983. 193p.
Leifer looks at the East Timor issue as seen from Jakarta, placing it within the context
of Indonesia's foreign policy at that time and the maintenance of a regional order.

202 War and diplomacy: the Timor case.
Hamish McDonald. In: *Suharto's Indonesia*. By Hamish McDonald.
Melbourne, Australia: Fonata/Collins, 1980, p. 189–215. map.
A concise general account of conflict in East Timor from the time of the Armed Forces
Movement coup in Lisbon in April 1974, through invasion in December 1975 and
integration as the 27th Indonesian province in July 1976 to the continuing guerilla war
waged by Fretilin forces. It is particularly strong on the affairs within the Indonesian
camp, especially the army and the diplomatic initiatives.

203   **The struggle for East Timor.**
Sue Nichterlein.   Part 1 (1978, 50p) and part 2 (1979, 51p), New York:
The Author.
The author worked for the Fretilin representation to the United Nations in New York
and has done important research work on the situation in the territory. Here she lets
her Fretilin sympathies show.

204   **Timor: the stillborn nation.**
Bill Nicol.   Melbourne, Australia; Norwalk, Connecticut: Visa, 1978.
328p. maps. bibliog.
The author is an Australian journalist who reported from East Timor in 1975. His
book can be divided into five sections: history and Portuguese background, the
political situation in 1974 and 1975, the rôle of the Portuguese, how Indonesia and
Australia reacted to these political developments and how these factors came together
in civil war and invasion.

205   **The East Timor conflict and western response.**
Torben Retbøll.   *Bulletin of Concerned Asian Scholars*, vol. 19, no. 1
(Jan. 1987), p. 24–49. map.
A consideration of the situation in East Timor between December 1975 and the end of
1985, covering the struggle against Indonesian occupation, human rights violations and
foreign visitors. The attitudes of the United States, Britain, Australia, Portugal,
Holland and Sweden are successively considered, as are the rôles of international relief
agencies, the Catholic church and the United Nations.

206   **East Timor, Indonesia and the western democracies: a collection of
documents.**
Edited by Torben Retbøll.   Copenhagen: Documentation Department
of the International Work Group for Indigenous Affairs, 1980. 138p.
maps. bibliog. (IWGIA Document, no. 40).
A collection of newspaper and periodical articles and other official documents designed
primarily to highlight human rights atrocities in East Timor, but also to point out the
complicity of Western governments in the affair and the rôle that the Western mass
media played in covering up the events. The collection opens and closes with United
Nations testimonies by Noam Chomsky, and is of particular use for research purposes
in that the articles are arranged by topic and origin rather than in chronological order.

207   **East Timor and Indonesia.**
Torben Retbøll.   *Bulletin of Concerned Asian Scholars*, vol. 15, no. 2
(April 1983), p. 59–61.
A short report on the most up-to-date information at the time, specifically a report
from the Regional People's Assembly of East Timor to President Suharto in summer
1981 which says 'after 5 years of integration, the people of East Timor do not yet enjoy
the freedom that humanity needs to feel'. There is an account of a new Indonesian
military offensive in Timor at that time.

208 **East Timor: the struggle continues.**
Edited by Torben Retbøll. Copenhagen: Documentation Department of the International Work Group for Indigenous Affairs, 1984. 212p. maps. bibliog. (IWGIA Document, no. 50).

This book is a sequel to *East Timor, Indonesia and the western democracies* (q.v.). The earlier report covered the conflict from the Indonesian invasion in 1975 until the end of 1979, this new report concentrates largely on developments since 1980. Once again there is a selection of articles and official documents arranged according to topic and source, including a chapter on Sweden, as well as the Roman Catholic church, Australia, the United Nations and the International Committee for the Red Cross. There is also a specially prepared chapter *The people of East Timor and their struggle for survival*, which helps to place the events in East Timor in historical and cultural perspective.

209 **Timor Timur: 27a província da Indónesia.** (Timor Timur: 27th province of Indonesia).
Nuno Rocha. Lisbon: Nova Nórdica, 1987. 222p.

This Portuguese journalist was flown to East Timor as a guest of the Indonesian Foreign Minister. Here he puts the Indonesian case to the Portuguese public.

210 **East Timor: unfinished business.**
Southeast Asian Chronicle, no. 94 (June 1984), 28p. bibliog.

This special edition given over to East Timor is an upbeat account of Fretilin's continuing fight against the Indonesians, with articles on Fretilin and its growth, life during the occupation, the charges against Indonesia, and diplomatic efforts to cease the conflict. An excellent resource guide with bibliography, list of publications and campaigning organizations.

211 **The conquest of East Timor.**
Keith D. Suter. *Contemporary Review*, vol. 232, no. 1346 (March 1978), p. 134–41.

Discusses the Indonesian invasion, the development of the liberation movement, Fretilin and international reactions, concentrating on political and miltary events from 1974 to 1977.

212 **East Timor and West Irian.**
Keith D. Suter. London: Minority Rights Group, 1982. 2nd ed. 24p. map. bibliog. (Minority Rights Group Report 42).

Describes East Timor's transition from colony to independence to Indonesian invasion and efforts to protect human rights.

213 **The military situation in East Timor.**
Richard Tanter. *Pacific Research*, vol. 8, no. 2 (Jan.–Feb. 1977),
p. 1–6. map.
An account of Fretilin and Indonesian fighting after eighteen months of invasion,
dealing in generalities and very poor on details. Mainly based on Fretilin sources and
Australian press reports. The article also appeared reprinted in *Dissent*, no. 35–36
(May 1977), p. 3–9.

214 **The Indonesian occupation of East Timor, 1974–1989: a chronology.**
John G. Taylor. London: Catholic Institute for International
Relations Research with the Refugee Studies Programme, University of
Oxford, 1990. 95p. map.
The chronology begins eighteen months before the Indonesian invasion and focuses on
the demise of Portuguese colonialism and the emergence of a Fretilin administration.
The subsequent events of the Indonesian invasion are catalogued in full, as are details
of international reactions to the annexation. Of particular use is a listing of Indonesian
and Portuguese-language press articles in translation.

215 **Indonesia's forgotten war: the hidden history of East Timor.**
John G. Taylor. London: Zed, 1991. 215p. map. bibliog.
A comprehensive account of the situation in East Timor between April 1974 and April
1990. The author describes Indonesia's military campaigns, the human rights situation,
social conditions, and discusses reasons for Western complicity. Of particular interest
are his theories on the reasons for the continued resistance campaign by the Timorese
against great odds and a discussion of various possible outcomes of the situation.

216 **Portuguese Timor: an Indonesian dilemma.**
Donald E. Weatherbee. *Asian Survey*, vol. 6, no. 12 (Dec. 1966),
p. 683–95.
Weatherbee examines Portuguese Timor as a problem for Indonesian foreign policy,
providing some insights into the determinants of Indonesia's approach to Portuguese
imperialism in the archipelago. The author concludes by saying that 'in a sense
Portuguese Timor is a trust territory, the Portuguese holding it in trust for Indonesia'.

Southeast Asia's second front: the power struggle in the Malay archipelago.
See item no. 59

Timor: da ocupação japonesa a ocupação indonesia. (Timor: from Japanese
occupation to Indonesian occupation.)
See item no. 64.

Indonesia: an alternative history.
See item no. 68.

I am Timorese: testimonies from East Timor.
See item no. 181.

Feto Rai Timor. Mulheres de Timor. (Women of Timor.)
See item no. 183.

Indonesia's newest minority: the East Timorese.
See item no. 184

Indonesia's annexation of East Timor: political, administrative and developmental initiatives.
See item no. 185.

East Timor: beyond hunger: analysis of famine, 1979–1980.
See item no. 189.

The Indonesianization of East Timor.
See item no. 190.

The redundancy of courage.
See item no. 296.

1974–75

217 **East Timor.**
Cees van Dijk. *Review of Indonesian and Malaysian Affairs*, vol. 10, no. 1 (Jan.–June 1976). p. 1–31.
A good, well-balanced article, based primarily on Indonesian newspaper articles, covering events from April 1974 to January 1976. History, political parties, Australian and Indonesian attitudes, Portuguese mediatory efforts and foreign intervention are all dealt with.

218 **Portuguese Timor: the independence movement from coalition to conflict.**
James Stanley Dunn. *Dyason House Papers*, vol. 2, no. 1 (August 1975), p. 1–3.
Looks at the coalition between Fretilin and UDT in early 1975 which 'seemed to presage a rational and positive step towards the emergence of a new state . . .'. The author claims the coalition was always fragile, being held together only by apprehension at the Indonesian campaign against independence and continuing political crisis in Portugal.

219 **De l'évolution de divers territoires de l'ancien outre-mer portugais.** (On the political evolution of several former Portuguese overseas territories.)
André Durieux. *Bulletin des Séances de l'Academie des Sciences d'Outre-mer*, vol. 26, no. 3 (1980), p. 357–76.
Traces the political development of four small former Portuguese colonies since the Portuguese revolution of April 1974. Portuguese India (Goa) has been incorporated into India and East Timor into Indonesia. São Tomé and Principle are independent, and Macao remains a Portuguese territory.

220 **Timor: freedom caught between the powers.**
Denis Freney. Nottingham, England: Spokesman, 1975. 68p. map.
A formulaic work on East Timor, describing Portuguese, American and Australian connivance in the events with a tone of moral indignation. It is rather predictable in its apportioning of blame. Written only six weeks after the UDT coup it focuses on these events and the feud between UDT and Fretilin, it tries to establish why it took place.

221 **East Timor: civil war – causes and consequences.**
J. Stephen Hoadley. *Southeast Asian Affairs*, 1976, p. 411–19.
For those wishing to look a bit deeper into the political wranglings of the UDT–Fretilin coalition that degenerated into civil war, this is somewhat more detailed and critical than most accounts. The author apportions blame for the events to each of the Timorese parties for the arrogance of claiming a majority of popular support, with the UDT for breaking off the coalition, with Fretilin for not attending the Macao summit, with Portugal for not taking the Timorese party leaders seriously and with Indonesia for taking Fretilin rhetoric too seriously.

222 **The future of Portuguese Timor: dilemmas and opportunities.**
J. Stephen Hoadley. Institute of Southeast Asian Studies, Singapore, 1975. 28p. map. (Occasional paper, no. 27).
Appearing in March 1975 this paper assesses the first year of Timorese party politics without the hindsight of the Indonesian invasion, concluding that a Timorese-led government, responsible and responsive to the needs of the various ethnic and economic groups would be less likely to give rise to conflict than an Indonesian government responsive to Jakarta.

223 **Portuguese Timor and regional stability.**
J. Stephen Hoadley. *Southeast Asian Spectrum*, vol. 3, no. 4 (July 1975), p. 1–14.
In this SEATO publication the author gives a detailed account of the various political forces at work in Portuguese Timor at the time of writing. After the fall of the Caetano régime in Portugal in April 1974 and the subsequent growth of local political parties in Timor, there was an upsurge in regional interest in the colony. The coalition was running smoothly at that time and the author suggests some economic and political linkages in the region that could have helped East Timor to remain a viable nation.

224 **The eyewitness: bitter moments in East-Timor jungles.**
Arsenio Ramos Horta. Singapore: Usaha Quality Printers, [n.d.]. 76p.
Indicative of the parochial nature of East Timorese politics, this is a fiercely anti-Fretilin account of the coup and the civil war from the brother of José Manuel Ramos Horta, the Fretilin diplomat at the United Nations.

225 **Indonesia and East Timor: the politics of phased annexation.**
Justus M. van der Kroef. *Solidarity*, vol. 10, no. 5–6 (Sept.–Dec. 1976), p. 17–28.
Describes the Indonesian handling of the East Timor affair from 1974 until the integration of the territory in July 1976 and their attempts to convince the world that the merger has taken place according to the wishes of the people of East Timor.

226 **The Indonesian takeover of East Timor.**
Robert Lawless. *Asian Survey*, vol. 16, no. 10 (Oct. 1976), p. 948–64. map.
Lawless examines the politics involved in Indonesia's takeover of East Timor, 1974–76, including the rôle of the United Nations, the struggle of small ethnic groups and the collapse of colonialism into what the author calls 'regional imperialism'.

227 **The struggle for East Timor: prelude to invasion.**
Sue Nichterlein. *Journal of Contemporary Asia*, vol. 7, no. 4 (1977), p. 486–96.
Political events in 1974 and 1975 before the invasion are analysed here, based on a number of different sources, the major Indonesian source being the daily newspaper *Sinar Harapan*.

228 **Relatórios da descolonização de Timor I: relatório do governor de Timor (periódo de 13 de Novembro de 1974 a 7 de Dezembro de 1975).** (Report on the decolonization of Timor I: report of the governor of Timor [from 13 November 1974 to 7 December 1975].)
Mário Lemos Pires. Lisbon: Presidência do Conselho de Ministros, 1981. 378p.
This is the official report of the Portuguese governor at the time of decolonization and invasion. It covers the situation in East Timor between November 1974, when Lemos Pires took office, and May 1975, the Macau meeting in May–July 1975, the UDT coup, the flight of the Portuguese administration to Ataúro, the formation of a government in Ataúro and the Indonesian invasion. There are large documentary annexes.

229 **Timor – 1: no changes overnight.**
Stephen R. Ranck. *New Guinea and Australia; the Pacific and Southeast Asia*, vol. 10, no. 1 (May–June 1975), p. 17–29.
Written after nearly a year of party politics in East Timor, this is a good insight into the different ethnic groups' attitudes to the political changes in the region.

230 **Relatórios da descolonização de Timor II: relatório da Commisão de Analíse e Esclarecimento do Processo de Descolonização de Timor.**
(Report on the decolonization of Timor II: report from the commission of analysis and explanation on the process of decolonization of Timor.)
Francisco A. Riscado, Paula Vicente, João Gonlão de Melo, Carlos S.C. Pecorelli. Lisbon: Presidência do Conselho de Ministros, 1981. 301p.
The report of a Portuguese parliamentary commission set up to look into the process of decolonization, beginning in April 1974.

Australia and New Zealand

231 **New Zealand's response to the East Timor controversy.**
J. Stephen Hoadley. *New Zealand International Review*, vol. 1, no. 6 (Nov.–Dec. 1976), p. 4–8.
From 1974 until September 1976 little interest was shown in New Zealand over the East Timor question. Towards the end of that period, New Zealand had formally accepted that East Timor was part of Indonesia, agreeing with the Indonesian viewpoint that the matter is an internal Indonesian affair and not a subject of debate before an international forum.

232 **The impact of the ABC on Australian–Indonesian relations since Timor.**
Errol Hodge. *Australian Journal of International Affairs*, vol. 45, no. 1 (May 1991), p. 109–22.
Examines the way in which the reporting of events in East Timor to Radio Australia's millions of listeners in Indonesia created a serious rift between Jakarta and Canberra.

233 **East Timor: from beginning to end.**
George J. Munster. In: *Secrets of state.* By George J. Munster. Sydney: Walsh & Munster, 1982. p. 65–89. 168p.
Discusses the advice given by senior Australian public servants in the prelude to invasion, especially the ambassador to Jakarta at that time, Richard Woolcott, and the first secretary of the strategic and international policy division of the Australian defence department, W.B. Pritchett.

234 **Australia: courtier or courtesan? The Timor issue revisited.**
Sue Nichterlein. *Australian Outlook*, vol. 36, no. 1 (April 1982). p. 46–50.
A brief but very detailed look at Australia's rôle in the Indonesian annexation of East Timor, critical of Australia's official attitudes to developments in East Timor between 1974 and 1980. According to the author Australia forsook its chance to become a major regional power in diplomatic terms, losing its moral and political credibility.

Indonesian Invasion and Foreign Relations. Australia and New Zealand

235 The human rights and conditions of the people of East Timor.
Senate Standing Committee on Foreign Affairs and Defence.
Canberra: Australian Government Publishing Service, 1983. 106p.
This is an Australian Government enquiry into the human rights and conditions of the people of Timor and the appropriate policies to be adopted by an Australian Government in relation to matters revealed in the Committee's enquiry.

236 Process and picture: East Timor.
Rodney Tiffen. In: *The news from southeast Asia. The sociology of newsmaking.* By Rodney Tiffen. Singapore: Institute of Southeast Asian Studies, 1978, p. 160–81.
The book from which this chapter is taken focuses on the social processes of newsmaking, this chapter showing how these affect the picture of Southeast Asia conveyed through news coverage. Presented here is a case study of Australian press coverage of East Timor. The types of information channels through which information reached reporters are discussed, followed by an examination of the way in which antagonistic relations between the Indonesian government and reporters developed. Finally, the way East Timor developed as an issue on the Australian political agenda and the ways in which this related to news coverage are examined.

237 Australians and the East Timor issue.
Nancy Viviani. *Australian Outlook*, vol. 30, no. 2 (August 1976), p. 197–226.
Looks at the interaction of Australian government policy and domestic opinion in Australia on the Timor issue and makes an attempt to define the impact of these conflicts on future Australian–Indonesian relations.

238 Australia, Indonesia and Europe's empires.
Edward Gough Whitlam. *Australian Outlook*, vol. 34, no. 1 (April 1980), p. 3–12.
Deals with Australian–Indonesian policy from 1948 onwards, especially in relation to the Netherlands and Portugal, concerning West New Guinea and East Timor respectively. The article sketches the development of Australian–Indonesian relations, which were rather tense at the time, and the sequence and interaction of political and military events.

239 Indonesia and Australia: political aspects.
Edward Gough Whitlam. In: *Indonesia, the making of a nation.* Edited by J.A.C. Mackie. Canberra: Australian National University, Research School of Pacific Studies. 1980, p. 756–66.
A concise history of Indonesian–Australian relations since 1949, and a detailed account of the Australian position in the run-up to the Indonesian invasion. The tone of the piece is pro-Indonesian with an attempt to steer the blame well away from Australia, citing 'the irresponsibility of the Portuguese' and claiming the name of Fretilin's proclaimed 'Democratic Republic of East Timor' 'had overtones of East Germany, North Korea and North Vietnam'.

Portugal and Europe

240   The Timor drama.
João Loff Barreto.   Lisbon: Timor Newsletter, 1982. 60p.

The author, a lawyer, presented this paper, based on research in Portuguese archives and previously unpublished sources to the Permanent People's Tribunal which met in Lisbon in June 1981. The author describes the position of the Portuguese government in the crucial twenty months between April 1974 and December 1975. The Portuguese media responded emotively to the testimony at the Tribunal, in some cases arguing that the political personalities involved had been unjustly treated. The author sent his report to those mentioned in the report and replies are printed in an appendix.

241   East Timor and the shaming of the West.
Alexander George.   London: Tapol, 1985. 60p. map.

Focuses on the policies of the British goverment, contrasting private policies and public statements. Cites the case of the Labour government arguing that they had played a leading part in efforts to reach an internationally acceptable settlement in East Timor, having just agreed to sell eight Hawk ground-attack aircraft to Indonesia two months earlier.

242   Osttimor – das vergessene Sterben: Indonesicher Völkermord unter Ausschluß der Weltöffentlichkeit. (East Timor – the forgotten dead: Indonesian genocide hidden from the world.)
Klemens Ludwig, Korinna Horta. Foreword by Bishop Franz Kamphans.   Göttingen, Germany: Gesellschaft für bedrohte Völker, 1985. 152p. map. (Reihe Bedrohte Völker Taschenbuch 1013).

Contains much of the usual information and discussion but also a useful chapter on West Germany's place in the conflict.

243   O problema político de Timor. (The political problem of Timor.)
Luís Filipe F.R. Thomaz.   Braga, Portugal: Editora Pax, 1975. 142p.

244   Timor, autopsia de uma tragédia. (Timor: autopsy of a tragedy.)
Luís Filipe F.R. Thomaz.   Lisbon: DIG/Livro, 1977. 175p.

This and the previous entry are the works of a historian who completed his military service in Timor where he played a small rôle during decolonization. The author gives details of Fretilin human rights violations.

Timor: a people betrayed.
See item no. 193.

The East Timor conflict and western response.
See item no. 205.

United Nations

245 **East Timor: a study in decolonization.**
Robert Crawford, Perumala Dayanidhi. *India Quarterly*, vol. 33, no.
4 (Oct.–Dec. 1977), p. 419–31.
The authors claim that although the issue of East Timor has failed to attract the wide
attention which other decolonizations have enjoyed, it nevertheless holds significance
for the student of international politics, because of its ramifications for the
decolonization process as a whole and for the light which it sheds on the rôle played by
political and ideological factors in the procedure. In addition, the way in which the
United Nations has dealt with this issue has illustrated certain long-standing trends
affecting the organization.

246 **Funu. (War.)**
José Ramos Horta.   Trenton, New Jersey: Red Sea, 1987. 207p. map.
Ramos Horta is one of the few Fretilin officials who had left East Timor prior to the
Indonesian invasion in 1975, and has long served as Fretilin's representative at the
United Nations in New York. This semi-autobiographical account of the events leading
up to the invasion is important for its original insights into diplomatic efforts.

247 **O drama de Timor: relatório da ONU sobre a descolonização.** (The
Timor drama: United Nations report on decolonization.)
Adriano Moreira.   Lisbon: Intervenção, 1977. 106p. map.
A translation of a United Nations document, accompanied by commentary by this
Portuguese ex-overseas minister under Salazar.

248 **Decolonization no. 7.**
United Nations.   New York: United Nations Department of Political
Affairs, Trusteeship and Decolonization, 1976. 71p. map.
A thorough report on the political evolution in Portuguese Timor, the ensuing civil
war, Indonesian intervention and military and political developments between January
and June 1976. Naturally, it is very good on the situation in the United Nations and the
international arena.

The East Timor conflict and western response.
See item no. 205.

United States

249 **Benign terror: East Timor.**
Noam Chomsky, Edward Herman.   *Bulletin of Concerned Asian
Scholars*, vol. 11, no. 2, (April–June 1979), p. 40–68. maps. bibliog.
The first part of this article deals with the semantics of terror and violence, discussing
the way in which human rights atrocities can be accounted for in the fight against

'terrorism', which has restricted the sense to the retail violence of those who oppose the established order. The authors hold up Indonesia as an example, claiming it has been able to commit atrocities in East Timor with the connivance of the West by playing on fears of a 'terrorist power-base' in the former Portuguese colony. Beyond that the article is a formulaic piece on the invasion. This is an abridged version of the third chapter of Noam Chomsky and Edward Herman's *The Washington connection and third world fascism* (Boston, Massachusetts: South End, 1979), which has a longer discussion on the semantics and examples of terror regimes in other countries.

250 **East Timor: the responsibility of the United States.**
Richard W. Franke. *Bulletin of Concerned Asian Scholars*, vol. 15, no. 2 (April–June 1983), p. 42–58. map.
These papers were presented to the Permanent People's Tribunal in Lisbon in June 1981. The author argues that the United States supplied military aid vital in the invasion and occupation of East Timor, United States diplomatic resources were put at the disposal of the Indonesians in 1975, the United States supported Indonesia at the United Nations and the United States attempted to deceive and abuse public opinion and manipulate and control humanitarian aid to East Timor.

251 **The United States and genocide in East Timor.**
Scott Sidell. *Journal of Contemporary Asia*, vol. 11, no. 1 (1981), p. 44–61.
Discusses the political evolution of East Timor, human rights conditions in the territory and United States strategic interests in the region. According to the article, United States military equipment delivered to the government of Indonesia has significantly contributed to the death or starvation of hundreds of thousands of inhabitants of East Timor. Despite repeated United Nations condemnation of Indonesia, such military aid has increased.

East Timor: beyond hunger: analysis of famine, 1979–1980.
See item no. 189.

The East Timor conflict and western response.
See item no. 205.

Indonesian accounts

252 **Decolonization in East Timor.**
Department of Foreign Affairs. Jakarta: Republic of Indonesia, Department of Foreign Affairs, 1976. 37p. map.
This document gives an official Indonesian version of the background to the situation in East Timor from the time of the Portuguese revolution in April 1974 to the proclamation of the 27th Indonesian province of Timor Timur in July 1976. There is an annex containing facsimiles of correspondence between the United Nations and the Indonesian permanent representative, Indonesian Red Cross reports into human rights violations committed by Fretilin, the formalization of the integration of East Timor

into Indonesia and the Balibo declaration in which four of the East Timorese political parties, UDT, KOTA, APODETI and Partido Trabalhista, requested Indonesian involvement in events in the province in November 1975.

253 **Government statements on the East Timor question.**
Department of Information.   Jakarta: Republic of Indonesia,
Department of Information, 1975. 25p.
A collection of five Indonesian government statements over the period 4–22 December 1975 with regard to the situation in East Timor at that time and the Indonesian invasion. 'With these developments the Indonesian government was given no alternative but to let the Indonesian volunteers follow their desire to help their brethren free themselves from colonial suppression and Fretilin terror.'

254 **The process of decolonization in East Timor.**
Department of Information.   Jakarta: Republic of Indonesia,
Department of Information, 1976. 40p.
Among the carefully chosen words and objective statement of fact in this Indonesian account of events at the takeover there is the claim that 'it was difficult for the Indonesian government to prevent the volunteers from protecting the refugees who were returning to their homeland and from assisting their brothers to free themselves from Fretilin's terror, oppression and highhandedness'.

255 **The question of Portuguese Timor.**
Department of Information.   Jakarta: Republic of Indonesia,
Department of Indonesia, 1975. 40p. map.
A discussion of Portuguese politics, the Macau conference, and civil war ending with the meeting of foreign ministers from Indonesia and Portugal in Rome in early November 1975.

256 **The decolonization of East Timor: a historical review.**
Kristiadi.   *The Indonesian Quarterly*, vol. 14, no. 4 (1986), p. 546–77.
The author, a staff member of the Official Centre for Strategic and International Studies (SIS) which publishes the *Quarterly*, deals principally with the 1974–75 period from a pro-Indonesian point of view.

257 **Integrasi: kebulatan tekad rakyat Timor Timur.** (Integration: the unanimous will of the East Timorese people.)
Compiled by Soekanto.   Jakarta: Yayasan Parikesit, 1976. 714p. map.
A detailed account of the Timor crisis as seen from Jakarta, with many copies of official statements, agreements, communiqués and photographs.

Human Rights and International Law

258 **East Timor: violations of human rights: extrajudicial executions, 'disappearances', torture and political imprisonment, 1975–1984.**
Amnesty International. London: Amnesty International Publications, 1985. 92p. maps.

A detailed report on alleged abuse of human rights by Indonesian forces following the invasion of December 1975. Despite being denied access to the territory Amnesty International claims to have accumulated a large body of information on its concerns in East Timor. Some of this information is documentary, comprising published reports, accounts written and passed to Amnesty International in confidence and other confidential material, including copies of interrogation reports by the Indonesian authorities. The report covers specific case histories of disappearances, execution and torture and provides detailed lists of victims of human rights abuse. There is also information about Indonesia's response to allegations made against it and the efforts of Amnesty International, the International Committee of the Red Cross and other international relief agencies to monitor the situation in East Timor more closely.

259 **The decolonization of East Timor and the United Nations norms of self-determination and aggression.**
Roger S. Clark. *The Yale Journal of World Public Order*, vol. 7, no. 1 (Autumn 1980), p. 2–44.

A precise analysis of the legal issues at stake: 'expressions of will', 'universal adult suffrage', 'processes impartially conducted', 'full knowledge', 'advanced stage of self-government', 'historic, ethnic and cultural ties between Indonesia and East Timor'. The author also covers some of the legal bases of Indonesian claims: the Western Sahara Option, economic viability, armed aggression, self-defence, invitation by the East Timorese, long-term regional security and humanitarian intervention.

260 **Does the Genocide Convention go far enough? Some thoughts on the nature of criminal genocide in the context of Indonesia's invasion of East Timor.**
Roger S. Clark. *Ohio Northern University Law Review*, vol. 8, no. 2 (1981), p. 321–28.

The author suggests expanding the United Nations Genocide Convention to include reckless and negligent genocide. He sets the scene with a description of events during the invasion and then offers some thoughts about criminal guilt as it applies to genocide in its criminal sense.

261 **East Timor and international law.**
Roger S. Clark. *Mennesker og Rettigheter*, vol. 2, no. 1 (1984), p. 32–34.

Discusses some legal issues raised by the invasion of East Timor. According to the author Indonesia violated two fundamental norms of international law: it deprived East Timor of its right to self-determination and the military intervention of the Indonesian army constituted an act of aggression forbidden by the United Nations Charter and customary law.

262 **The East Timor dispute.**
Paul D. Elliott. *The International and Comparative Law Quarterly*, vol. 27, no. 1 (Jan. 1978), p. 238–49.

The conflict in East Timor has raised many international law issues. The aim of this note is to concentrate upon the effect of the dispute on the status and application of the principle of self-determination. The factual background to the events is given, as well as the actions of the United States and the arguments for Indonesia. The principle of self-determination is introduced and discussed in terms of the East Timor's present situation.

263 **Fretilin massacres: testimonies of the survivors from Fretilin massacres.**
Edited by José Maria Costa de Freitas, translated by Arsenio Ramos Horta. Singapore: Usaha Quality Printers, [n.d.]. 48p.

Describes the experiences of four witnesses and victims of alleged human rights violations by Fretilin.

264 **East Timor and self-determination.**
The Review, International Commission of Jurists, no. 32 (June 1984), p. 1–6.

Some background information on the political and military events between 1974 and 1983, raising two questions: was armed intervention legally justifiable, and did the people of East Timor participate in a genuine act of self-determination?

265 **East Timor: the problem and the human rights polemic (1).**
Justus M. van der Kroef. *Asian Thought and Society*, vol. 7, no. 21
(Nov. 1982), p. 240–63.

The discussion starts from 24 November 1981 when the United Nations General
Assembly once again adopted a resolution affirming the right to self-determination of
the population of East Timor and urging prompt aid by member nations to meet the
problem of reported famine in the region. This article discusses some of the political
changes after more than five years of integration, calling into question the inevitability
of a Timorese government fronted by Fretilin as proposed by some observers, e.g.
Jolliffe (q.v.). The author says it would have been likely that the moderate UDT
elements would have emerged as most 'representative' of East Timor's wishes at the
time in any fair act of self-determination.

266 **East Timor: the problem and the human rights polemic (2).**
Justus M. van der Kroef. *Asian Thought and Society*, vol. 8, no.
22–23 (March 1983), p. 72–93.

Discusses Australian affairs and The Netherlands, China, Vietnam. Despite ongoing
problems he says the issues for many East Timorese are the development prospects of
their region and whether that development is best achieved under Indonesian rule with
an occasional spotlight of embarrassing revelation to goad Jakarta on, or as yet another
mini-state at the mercy of international power and commodity market forces. In the
author's opinion it must be said for the region's needs the Indonesian annexation may
well be the best possible long-term development matrix.

267 **International law and East Timor.**
Keith D. Suter. *Dyason House Papers*, vol. 5, no. 2 (Dec. 1978),
p. 1–10.

A useful introduction to the international law issues concerning East Timor, grouped
under the headings: Indonesian invasion of East Timor; United Nations actions;
conduct of the Indonesian military campaign; Australia's recognition of Indonesian
control over East Timor and East Timor as an 'internal' Indonesian matter. In general
terms Indonesia comes out of this examination as having broken a number of
international law provisions. The author maintains that, while the lack of agreed
information makes any final judgement very difficult, especially on particular incidents
and allegations, the overall pattern is one of a country which has flouted international
law.

East Timor: a christian reflection. Timor Oriental: une reflexion chrétienne.
See item no. 170.

Feto Rai Timor. Mulheres de Timor. (Women of Timor.)
See item no. 183.

Indonesia's newest minority : the East Timorese.
See item no. 184.

Benign terror: East Timor.
See item no. 249.

Human Rights and International Law

Amnesty International Report.
See item no. 334.

Tapol Bulletin.
See item no. 357.

The Economy and Economic Development

Colonial

268 **Timor: a primeira terra portuguesa aquém da 'barreira do tempo'.**
(Timor: the first Portuguese land on this side of the International Date
Line).
Viriato Campos.   Lisbon: Agência Geral do Ultramar, 1967. 52p.
A collection of articles previously published in the Portuguese newspaper *Diário de
Lisboa*, dealing with António de Abreu, development of health services, education,
public works and road construction.

269 **Timor: ante-câmara do inferno!?** (Timor: ante-chamber of hell!?)
Teófilo Duarte.   Famalicão, Portugal: 'Minerva', de Gaspar Pinto de
Sousa e Irmão, 1930. 409p. map.
A former governor examines many aspects of Portuguese Timor, with
the emphasis on trade and administration.

270 **Asian trade and European influence in the Indonesian archipelago
between 1500 and about 1630.**
Marie Antoinette Petronella Meilink-Roelofsz.   The Hague, The
Netherlands: Martinus Nijhoff, 1962. 471p. bibliog.
Excellent, thoroughly researched, introduction to trade in the archipelago, with many
references to Timor including Javanese, Chinese, Portuguese traders and the
sandalwood trade.

271 **Chinese navigators in Insulinde about AD 1500.**
J.V. Mills. *Archipel*, no. 18 (1979), p. 69–93. map.
The main source of the routes to Timor followed by the Chinese navigators during the fifteenth century is the anonymous work entitled *Shun Fêng Hsiang Sung*, ('Fair Winds for Escort'). It includes navigational theory and practice, mnemonics and prayers and give notes on individual places along the sea route. Timor is the most southerly place mentioned, giving detailed instructions for passage from Patani and Banten to Timor, called Ch'ih-wên by the Chinese, who visited both the North and South coast of the island.

272 **The economic structure of an outpost in the outer islands in the Indonesian archipelago: Portuguese Timor, 1850–1975.**
Gerard J. Telkamp. In: *Between people and statistics: essays on modern Indonesian history presented to P. Creutzberg*. Edited by Francien van Anrooij, Dirk H.A. Kolff, Jan T.M. van Laanen, Gerard J. Telkamp. The Hague, The Netherlands: Martinus Nijhoff under the auspices of the Royal Tropical Institute, Amsterdam, 1979, p. 71–83. bibliog.
This is a concise survey of the political and general history of Portuguese Timor with some demographic information, an indication of the underdeveloped infrastructure and communications, a description of traditional subsistence agriculture, export crops and foreign trade.

Palms and the cross: socio-economic development in Nusatenggara, 1930–1975.
See item no. 178.

Post-colonial

273 **Key issues in Indonesian regional development.**
Iwan J. Azis. In: *Unity and diversity; regional economic development in Indonesia since 1970*. Edited by Hal Hill. Singapore: Oxford University Press, 1989, p. 55–74.
Explores some key issues in Indonesian regional development: the rôle of regional exports, interregional resource and budgetary allocations – together with the recent emphasis on decentralization – and trends in the concentration of industrial location. The analysis is primarily with reference to existing provincial boundaries, and thus deals with Nusa Tenggara Timur and Timor Timur.

274 **Kehidupan ekonomi penduduk di Timor Timur.** (The economic life of
the inhabitants of East Timor.)
Budhisantoso. *Berita Antropologi*, vol. 11, no. 36 (Jan.–March
1980), p. 82–107. bibliog.
A general survey of the East Timorese economy, with the emphasis on agriculture,
cattle breeding, handicrafts and trade. The article is based on secondary sources from
between 1929 and 1977.

275 **East and West Nusa Tenggara: isolation and poverty.**
Lorraine Corner. In: *Unity and diversity: regional development in
Indonesia since 1970.* Edited by Hal Hill. Singapore: Oxford University
Press, 1989, p. 178–206. map.
This contains much interesting and useful data for the province of which West Timor is
a part. It has sections on economic change between 1975–85, population, agriculture,
industry, trade, education, labour, provincial finance, key development problems and
the future.

276 **East Timor today.**
Department of Information. Jakarta: Department of Information,
1984. 89p. map.
In this pamphlet the Indonesian government details development aims and achieve-
ments in East Timor over the preceding decade, with many supporting facts and
figures. It focuses on domestic issues with a short piece on East Timor in the
international forum.

277 **Prospek pembangunan daerah Timor Timur.** (Prospects for the
development of East Timor.)
Hendra Esmara. *Prisma*, vol. 8, no. 7 (July 1979), p. 3–16. map.
The author puts his discussion within the context of the Indonesian five-year plan,
citing useful data and descriptions on Indonesian development efforts in the first three
years after integration, relying largely on official sources. He evaluates the hindrances
to development in East Timor, concluding that the population pattern is unsuitable and
that the day-to-day language of the territory must be changed to Indonesian. See also
Nusa Tenggara Timur: the challenges of development (edited by Colin Barlow, Alex
Bellis, Kate Andrews. Canberra: Australian National University, Dept of Political and
Social Change, 1991. 294p. [Political and Monographs, no. 12]).

278 **Regional development in Indonesia.**
Hal Hill, Anna Weidemann. In: *Unity and diversity: regional
economic development in Indonesia since 1970.* Edited by Hal Hill.
Singapore: Oxford University Press, 1989, p. 3–54.
An introduction to the dimensions of regional development in Indonesia. Although it
does not deal with Timor directly, it places East Nusa Tenggara and Timor Timur within
the Indonesian economy as a whole, indicating broad patterns – both similarities and
divergent trends, drawing attention to the trends at the sub-national level and examining
some major regional development issues in Indonesia. Tabular statistical material gives
information on GDP, population, labour, agriculture, manufacturing, investment,
expenditure, subsidies, cost of living, transport and exports for each province.

279 **An economic survey of East Nusatenggara.**
Willem H. Makaliwe, Ace Partadiredja. *Bulletin of Indonesian Economic Studies*, vol. 10, no. 1 (March 1974), p. 33–54.

A fair introduction to the economy of East Nusa Tenggara during the early seventies, covering regional income, provincial government budget, manufacturing, transport and communications. At the time of writing Nusa Tenggara was economically rather remote from the nation's centre, with much subsistence agriculture but a growing livestock industry.

280 **East Timor develops.**
Regional Government of East Timor. Dili: Regional Government of East Timor, 1984. 45p. map.

This glossy booklet provides information on economic development in East Timor, with many photographs and an upbeat text detailing some of the physical results.

281 **East Timor: questions of economic viability.**
M. Hadi Soesastro. In: *Unity and diversity: regional economic development in Indonesia since 1970*. Edited by Hal Hill. Singapore: Oxford University Press, 1989, p. 207–29. map.

As with Lorraine Corner's article on West and East Nusatenggara (q.v.) this contains much recent economic information. Following neglect by the Portuguese during colonial times and the devastating effect of invasion, the East Timorese economy was severely damaged. The author gives a brief economic history of the territory, and discusses the economic viability of East Timor in the light of recent economic and social developments.

Old lamps for new: recent developments in Nusa Tenggara Timur.
See item no. 177.

Palms and the cross: socio-economic development in Nusatenggara, 1930–1975.
See item no. 178.

Pasar dan integrasi di Timor Timur.
See item no. 188.

Dilemmas in introducing applied technology: the plough and the cattlelords in Timor.
See item no. 290.

Timor e a cultura do café. (Timor and coffee-growing.)
See item no. 293.

Timor Gap

282 **The zone of co-operation between Australia and Indonesia: a preliminary outline with particular reference to applicable law.**
H. Burmester. In: *Joint development of offshore oil and gas. Vol. 2..*
Edited by Hazel Fox. London: British Institute of International and
Comparative Law, 1990, p. 128–40. map.
Provides an outline of the negotiations and proposals for a zone of co-operation in the
Timor Gap and focuses particularly on issues of applicable law. The treaty between
Australia and Indonesia – 'Treaty between Australia and the Republic of Indonesia on
the zone of co-operation in an area between the Indonesian province of East Timor
and Northern Australia' – was signed by the foreign ministers of the respective
countries between the presentation of this paper and its publication. It is reproduced in
full in an annexe.

283 **Filling the gap – delimiting the Australia-Indonesia maritime boundary.**
Catriona Cook. *Australian Yearbook of International Law*, no. 10
(1987), p. 131–75. map.
A highly detailed legal treatment of the delimitation of Indonesian–Australian
boundaries, drawing on legal precedents to suggest some of the norms for its
delimitation.

284 **Australia/Indonesia Timor Gap zone of co-operation treaty: a new offshore petroleum regime.**
Garrie J. Moloney. *Journal of Energy and Natural Resources Law*,
vol. 8, no. 2 (1990), p. 128–41.
The author, explains how the Timor Gap treaty fits into the existing complex of
Australian and international law. There is a brief introduction to the treaty and the
exploration which led to its formulation.

Frontiers of Asia and Southeast Asia.
See item no. 33.

Agriculture

285 **Hunting and fishing in Timor.**
António dè Almeida. In: *Proceedings of the Ninth Pacific Science Congress, Bangkok, 1957. Vol. 3: Anthropological and social sciences.* Bangkok: Secretariat, Ninth Pacific Science Congress, 1963, p. 239–41.
These two activities not only provide important dietary supplements to the diets of the traditional Timorese swidden farmer but are also important social events. The Timorese traditionally hunted deer, boars and buffalo by burning an area of thicket and pursuing the animals as they flee. The Timorese are not great sailors and only a few catch fish in the rivers and the salt and freshwater lagoons that often lie behind the beaches, particularly on the south coast. The community on the island of Atauro, offshore from Dili, was traditionally a fishing community and there is a detailed description of their methods and equipment.

286 **Estudo das madeiras de Timor.** (A study of Timorese timbers.)
M. Clara P. Graça de Freitas. Lisbon: Ministério do Ultramar, Junta de Investigações do Ultramar, 1955–58. 2 vols. bibliog. (Mémorias, série botânica, no. 3; segunda série, no. 5).
Thirty-three tree species of potential timber use are described, with details of botanical affiliation, geographical distribution, commercial names and vernacular Timorese names. The timber is described in terms of its anatomical structure and uses for the timber trade.

287 **Agricultures timoraises.** (Timorese agriculture.)
Claudine Friedberg. *Études Rurales*, no. 53–56 (Jan.–Dec. 1974), p. 375–405. map.
In this comparative study the author tries to discover what relationships may exist among various ecological, technological, ritual and political aspects of certain Indonesian agricultural communities, in particular the Atoni, Bunak, Ema and the Southern Tetun and then compares them all with Java.

86

288 **The development of traditional agricultural practices in Western Timor from the ritual control of consumer goods production to the political control of prestige goods.**
Claudine Friedberg. In: *The evolution of social systems.* Edited by J. Friedman, M.J. Rowlands. London: Gerald Duckworth, 1977, p. 137–71. map.

Essentially a longer version of the above article, this first examines the way each community – Bunak, Ema, Tetun and Atoni – traditionally influenced the productivity of its territory through both technical and ritual means. The author then analyses the process of the accumulation of wealth in agricultural products on the one hand, and in those goods obtained through trade on the other.

289 **Social rituals of territorial management in light of Bunaq farming rituals.**
Claudine Friedberg. *Bijdragen tot de Taal-, Land- en Volkenkunde,* vol. 145, no. 4 (1989), p. 548–62. bibliog.

Agricultural rites may be considered to be a means of bringing into play that which a society deems necessary for controlling its livelihood and, thereby, its reproduction. Analysing the farming ritual cycle among the Bunak, several circuits of exchange are put forward by the author, who investigates how this ritual cycle works on several levels: the village as an autonomous unit; the house in which altar rites are performed and the agricultural field itself where rites are performed.

290 **Dilemmas in introducing applied technology: the plough and the cattlelords in Timor.**
Mary Johnston. *Community Development Journal,* vol. 25, no. 3 (July 1990), p. 243–51.

This welcome addition to development studies in Timor describes the reintroduction of the plough to Timor in 1974, and ensuing problems. It lists the social and technical problems of the traditional *luruk* system whereby cows were driven round the field to break up the mud.

291 **Lamtoro and the Amarasi model from Timor.**
Paul H. Jones. *Bulletin of Indonesian Economic Studies,* vol. 19, no. 3 (Dec. 1983), p. 106–12.

The author believes that the farming system which has evolved in the region of Amarasi in West Timor around the tree species *Leucaena leucocephala* is unique, has been largely overlooked and that its full potential as a replicable agroforestry model has not been fully appreciated. This paper describes the main features of the Amarasi model, examines replication prospects throughout Nusa Tenggara and explores its potential for raising living standards of people in tropical and sub-tropical mountainous areas where soils are poor and rainfall is low.

292 **Innovations in agriculture incorporating traditional production methods: the case of Amarasi (Timor).**
Joachim K. Metzner. *Bulletin of Indonesian Economic Studies*, vol. 19, no. 3 (Dec. 1983), p. 94–105. maps. bibliog.

This is an abridged version of an article published in *Applied Geography and Development*, (vol. 17, 1981) which details the agro-ecological change following the spread of *Lantana camara* over Amarasi in West Timor, causing a dramatic reduction in the numbers of livestock that could be grazed on the land. It proved good for shifting cultivators who could reduce their rotation cycles to two years' cultivation followed by between three and five fallow years. In Amarasi this shrub has been contained by the leguminous tree and shrub *Leucaena leucocephala* which is now prevalent.

293 **Timor e a cultura do café.** (Timor and coffee-growing.)
Helder Lains e Silva. Oporto, Portugal: Junta de Investigações do Ultramar, 1956. 196p. maps. bibliog. (Memórias, Junta de Investigações do Ultramar, Série de Agronomia Tropical, no. 1).

With the decline in sandalwood stocks in the nineteenth century the Portuguese moved into the production of high-grade coffee for export. This book covers not only the technical aspects of coffee production in Timor but is an important source of information on the owners of the coffee plantations, part of the social group which was to become an influential supporter of the UDT in the development of Timorese political parties in 1974. Coffee is still East Timor's most profitable commodity, all trade being controlled by a subsidiary company of the Indonesian army, P.T. Denok.

294 **Grasses of Portuguese Timor and information about their fodder value.**
Firmino António Soares. *Estudos Agronómicos*, vol. 4, no. 1 (Jan.–March 1963), p. 21–27.

Notes on eighty grasses, with field notes on their fodder value, based upon palatability for cattle.

Esboço histórico do sândalo no Timor Portûges. (An historical outline of sandalwood in Portuguese Timor.)
See item no. 46.

Reconhecimento preliminar das formações florestais no Timor Portûges. (A preliminary study of the forest types of Portuguese Timor.)
See item no. 48.

East and West Nusa Tenggara: isolation and poverty.
See item no. 275.

Literature and Linguistics

General

295 **Ruy Cinatti.**
Joaquim Manuel Magalhães.   Lisbon: Editorial Presença, 1986. 318p.
Ruy Cinatti Vaz Monteiro Gomes (1915–86), a poet with an established reputation in his native Portugal, published an important body of work concerning both cultural and scientific aspects of Timor. This selection of his poetry, chosen by Cinatti himself, contains works from all of the twenty-one collections he published between 1960 and 1984. Three collections dealt directly with his experience of Timor: *Uma sequência timorense* , 1970; *Timor-Amor*, and *Paisagens Timorenses com vultos*, both 1974. The poems are presented unannotated and without translations, but nevertheless, represent an important manifestation of Portuguese understanding and respect for Timor and her people and an interesting departure for those acquainted with Cinatti's other work.

296 **The redundancy of courage.**
Timothy Mo.   London: Chatto & Windus, 1991. 408p.
Based closely on the Indonesian invasion of East Timor and the armed struggle by the Timorese. The narrator is a homosexual Chinese hotel keeper who finds himself caught up in the conflict and taking to the mountains to join the guerilla campaign against the invading army. It is infinitely more successful at conveying the sense of personal tragedy, and human resilience, than the many academic and campaigning books and pamphlets.

East Timor: beyond hunger: analysis of famine, 1979–1980.
See item no. 189.

Oral literature

297 **Bei Gua, iténeraire de ancêtres: mythes des Bunaq de Timor.** (Bei Gua,
itinerary of ancestors: myths of the Bunak of Timor.)
Louis Berthe. Paris: Centre national de la recherche scientifique,
1972. 527p. maps. bibliog.

Oral literature is one of the most important literary forms in Timor and it has only
been transcribed in significant amounts during the past few decades. Traditionally, the
legends and myths are chanted or sung, containing many stylistic devices, repetition,
rhyme and alliteration, for example, which help the performer to memorize the verses.
The Bunak have one of the most elaborately developed traditions of narrative
recitation in Timor. This is a 7,400-verse genealogy of the Bunak, detailing the
formation of their society. It is presented here in full with French translation and
explanation. The author also describes the material culture, political and social
organization and other literary forms of the Bunak.

298 **Sur quelques distiques Buna' (Timor central).** (Concerning some
couplets of the Bunak [central Timor].)
Louis Berthe. *Bijdragen tot de Taal-, Land- en Volkenkunde*, no. 115
(1959), p. 337–71. bibliog.

The author introduces the reader to the traditional life of the Bunak, their annual cycle
of celebration and ritual and the place of song and verse in this cycle, for example,
during the rice harvest, funerals or at work and home. The *distiques* are reproduced in
the Bunak language with French translation, detailed linguistic description, phonology,
morphology, syntax and a glossary.

299 **Rythmes et genres dans las littérature orale des Fataluku de Lorehe
(Timor orientale), (Première partie).** (Rhythms and genres in Fataluku
oral literature from Lorehe [East Timor] [part 1].)
Maria Lameiras-Campagnolo, Henri Campagnolo. *L'Asic du Sud-Est
et Monde Insulindien*, vol. 10, no. 2–4 (1979), p. 19–48.

Aims at making an initial presentation of the rhythmic patterns of Fataluku oral
literature: metric when they are placed at forseeable poetic intervals (verses, stanzas
and fixed forms) and unmetrical ones in the opposite case (stories, genealogical
narratives).

300 **Adam and Eve on the island of Roti.**
James J. Fox. *Indonesia*, no. 36 (Oct. 1983), p. 15–23.

This article focuses on the recitation of an unusual chant in the ritual language of the
Rotinese, *Teke Telu ma Koa Hulu*, which the author reproduces and translates. He
illustrates how in this, a crucial Christian religious text, the story of Adam and Eve has
been transformed in the Rotinese oral tradition. He believes this to be illustrative of
the general process by which Christianity has been assimilated by the traditional
culture.

301 **Our ancestors spoke in pairs: Rotinese views of language, dialect and code.**
James J. Fox. In: *Explorations in the ethnography of speaking*. Edited by Richard Bauman, Joel Sherzer. Cambridge, England: Cambridge University Press, 1989, 2nd ed, p. 65–85. map.
The Rotinese speak the dialect of their own domain or *nusak* for everyday speech but orientate themselves to the entire island of Roti, with its dialect complexity, for the purpose of formal, ritual speech. The author discusses certain views the Rotinese hold of themselves, of their language, and of their dialects, and focuses these concepts in the examination of a single, islandwide form of speaking, a code used mainly in situations of formal interaction.

302 **Retelling the past: the communicative structure of a Rotinese historical narrative.**
James J. Fox. *Canberra Anthropology*, vol. 3, no. 1 (1976), p. 56–66. bibliog.
This is a comparison of two versions of the tale entitled *Oemau* from Roti. Although it is what the Rotinese call a 'true tale' these versions differ considerably. Approximately seventy years separate the two versions and, according to the author, they reflect the changed circumstances of the times, part of a creative process by which narratives are retold to maintain continuity with the past and yet account for changing circumstances of the present.

303 **To speak in pairs: essays on the ritual languages of eastern Indonesia.**
Edited by James J. Fox. Cambridge, England: Cambridge University Press, 1988. 338p. bibliog. (Cambridge Studies in Oral Literature, no. 15).
Traditional communication, both oral and written, among a large variety of peoples all over the world is characterized by the use of *parallelism*: sentences, words and clauses may correspond to each other as a result of the repetition of syntax. Of particular revelance is James J. Fox's *Manu Kama's road, Tepa Nilu's path*: *theme, narrative and formula in Rotinese ritual language.*

304 **Comment fut tranchée la liane celêste, et autre textes de littérature orale bunaq (Timor, Indonésie), recueillis et traduits par Louis Berthe.** (How the heavenly liana was cut and other texts from Bunak oral literature [Timor, Indonesia] collected and translated by Louis Berthe.)
Claudine Friedberg. Paris: Centre national de la recherche scientifique and the Conseil international de la langue française, 1978. 294p. maps. (Langues et Civilisations Tradition Orale, no. 25).
Because of its syntax and the fact that its vocabulary seems unrelated to those of neighbouring languages, Bunak has been assigned to the Papuan or non-austronesian linguistic group. However, the material presented in this work shows the difference is not as clear cut as it at first appears. The texts are also interesting from an ethnological angle.

305 **The Tetum folktale as a sociological, cosmological and logical model (Timor).**
David Hicks. *Anthropos* (Freiburg), no. 69, (1974), p. 57–67.
Three Tetun texts, involving crocodiles, dogs and sharks and monkeys, are given in English translation. The author's notes conclude that, in addition to its overt purpose of entertainment, the tales with monkeys as the main protagonists also serve as a vehicle for transmitting cultural values from one generation to the next.

306 **Myths and legends of Indonesia.**
Jan Knappert. Singapore: Heinemann Educational Books, 1977. 198p.
A school-level introduction to Indonesian culture, literature and language. Contains one story from Roti, *The prince*, which contains the memorable line: 'Goatskin, take me to the princess'.

307 **Head hunting in Timor and its historical implication.**
Pieter Middlekoop. University of Sydney, 1963. 423p. (Oceania Linguistic Monographs, no. 8a, b, c).
In this collection of texts dealing with warriorhood in western Timor, there is unfortunately very little explanation, the author choosing to allow the texts to speak for themselves.

308 **Migration of Timorese groups and the question of the kase metan or overseas black foreigners.**
Pieter Middlekoop. *Internationales Archiv für Ethnographie*, no. 51 (1968), p. 49–142. map. bibliog.
A very interesting, but rather opaque article, discussing three series of texts which deal with the influence that the Portuguese colonial settlements in Roti, Amarasi and Oecussi had on the migration of Timorese groups.

309 **Nai Tirans en Nai Besi in komische huwelijksrelatie met de krokodil.**
(Nai Tirans and Nai Besi in an amusing marriage with the crocodile.)
Pieter Middlekoop. *Bijdragen tot de Taal-, Land- en Volkenkunde*, no. 127, (1971), p. 434–51.
Discusses the myth of the origin of the land of Amarasi and the land of Roti, recorded in 1941 in Timor. In connection with the texts a variety of subjects are discussed, such as totem relations with the crocodile, the incest motif, the marriage between a virgin and a crocodile and the origin of the kings of the family of Nai Besi. The original text as well as a Dutch translation have been provided.

310 **A Timorese myth and three fables.**
Pieter Middlekoop. *Bijdragen tot de Taal-, Land- en Volkenkunde*, vol. 115 (1959), p. 157–75. bibliog.
Excellent transcription and translations collected by the author in West Timor, presented in parallel vernacular text with English translation. Some linguistic and cultural background notes are given. The author explains that Timorese fables are a

genre which have a tendency to fun. The attention is focused here on human experience in the form of meetings between animals and humans.

311 **Timor: legends and poems from the land of the sleeping crocodile. Book 1.**
H. Cliff Morris. Mulgrave, Australia: Waverley Offset Publishing Group, 1984. 209p.

A collection of poems and legends from East Timor presented in three Tetun dialects (Tetun-Belu, Tetun-Los and Tetun-Dili) with parallel English translations. They were all collected from Timorese people now resident outside Timor, the main intention being to allow Timorese people in all parts of the world to read in Tetun some of the stories in present day usage in Timor. Timor has a rich tradition of oral literature and the history of the island is related in the form of narrative legends. One such story is of a crocodile saved from death; in gratitude it turned itself into an island for the people who saved it. The island is Timor, the land of the sleeping crocodile.

312 **Uma lenda mambae.** (A Mambai legend.)
Frederico José Hopffer Rego. *Boletim de Sociedade de Geografia de Lisboa*, vol. 86, no. 4–6 (April–June 1968), p. 159–75.

The author gives a translation, with annotation, of a Mambai oral legend calling special attention to some details of ethnographic interest: various aspects of 'past/present' or 'remote past/more remote past' with possible allusive mention to first contacts of the Mambai with the Portuguese and Christianity.

313 **Textos em Teto da literatura oral timorense, volume 1.** (Tetun texts from Timorese oral literature.)
Artur Basílio de Sá. Lisbon: Junta de Investigações do Ultramar, Centro de Estudos Políticos e Sociais, 1961. 266p. (Estudos de Ciências Políticas e Sociais, no. 45).

Seven Tetun legends given in tran-literation and translation, including the arrival of the first priests and missionaries in Timor. Each legend is introduced and explained with linguistic notes.

314 **Oral literature of Indonesia.**
Edited by Subagio Sastrowardoyo, Sapardi Djoko Damono, A. Kasim Achmad. Jakarta: The Editors, sponsored by the ASEAN Committee on Culture and Information, 1985. 447p. map. (Anthology of Asean Literatures Volume 1a).

Four poems from Roti, collected by James J. Fox are given in parallel vernacular text and English translation. The first is a cautionary tale about baby Dela Kolik who is snatched from his mother and eaten by an eagle after she ate one of the eagle's eggs during her pregnancy. There are three examples of a poetry form called *bibi*.

Literature and Linguistics. Oral literature

315 **Volkssprookjes en legenden uit Indonesië.** (Folktales and legends from Indonesia.)
M. Prick van Wely.   Delft, The Netherlands: Elmar, 1978. 190p. bibliog.

This book contains two Timorese tales. In one of them the hero, with the unlikely name of Prince Michael, slays the seven-headed snake to win the hand of the princess from the neighbouring kingdom, and they all live happily ever after.

Literary masks and metaphysical truths: intimations from Timor.
See item no. 142.

Structural analysis in anthropology: case studies from Indonesia and Brazil.
See item no. 144.

Arts and Material Culture

General

316 **Cultural variations in eastern Indonesia (or, themes and variations in Nusa Tenggara Timur.)**
Marie Jeanne (Monni) Adams. *Manusia Indonesia*, vol. 5, no. 4–6 (1971), p. 425–40.
As an art historian the author spent almost two years on Sumba, Timor and Flores observing art forms, in particular their relationship to the local cultures. In this article she tries to clarify and order cultural elements in order to discover the interrelationships between the cultural elements of each island and to ascertain whether they are truly different features or variants of a kind.

317 **Notas sobre artes e ofícios de nativos de Timor Português.** (Notes on the arts and crafts of the natives of Portuguese Timor.)
António de Almeida. *Garcia de Orta*, vol. 7, no. 3 (1959), p. 445–51.
Covers various aspects of the economic and artistic products of the Timorese people. In discussing the arts and trade special reference is made to the production of cooking salt, pottery, weaving, rope work, carving of buffalo horn and houses, as well as gold, silver and brass work. There are thirty-six plates of fine photographs of handicrafts.

318 **Motivos artísticos timorenses e a sua integração.** (Timorese artistic motifs and their integration.)
Ruy Cinatti. Lisbon: Instituto de Investigação Científica Tropical, Museu de Etnologia, 1987. 189p.
As with Cinatti's *Arquitectura timorense* (q.v.) this work is both informative and beautifully illustrated. He introduces East Timor's cultural history and describes the various geometrical and figurative motifs and patterns used in the decoration of Timorese artefacts.

319 **Musikgeschichte in Bildern: Südostasien.** (A pictorial history of music: southeast Asia.)
Paul Collaer. Leipzig, Germany: VEB Deutscher Verlag für Musik Leipzig, 1979. 180p. map. bibliog.

The best Western-language account of Timorese music, mostly Eastern, with many photographs, detailed descriptions of instruments and an excellent bibliography. The only West Timorese instrument described is the *sesando* – made from the leaf of the lontar palm. The sesando deserves more attention as its resonator is very similar to the large calabashes used by the players of the *m'bira* in West Africa. It may be connected with the Topasses, who possibly included descendants of slaves brought from Portuguese West Africa. There is a short description of the *sesando* in *Presence and absence of Portuguese musical elements in Indonesia: an essay on the mechanism of musical acculturation* by Tilman Seebass (Durham, North Carolina: Duke University, 1988. 35p. map. bibliog. [Working Papers in Asian/Pacific Studies]).

320 **Sociological interpretation of differences in musical styles of the southern Tetun (Timor).**
Gérard Francillon. In: *Traditional drama and music of southeast Asia. Papers presented at the International Conference on Traditional Drama and Music of southeast Asia.* Edited by Mohammed Taib Osman. Kuala Lumpur: Dewan Bahasa dan Pustaka, 1974, p. 345–49.

This short paper proposes that the dualistic symbolic order is also represented in the music of West Timor. The author gives examples of the matrilineal Suai-Kamanasa, whose singing and dancing is rather restrained, and the Dirma who give vigorous performances.

321 **Art and religion on Timor.**
David Hicks. In: *Islands and ancestors: indigenous styles of southeast Asia.* Edited by Jean Paul Barbier, Douglas Newton, 1988. Munich: Prestel, p. 138–51. map.

Deals mainly with artefacts which have as their provenance central Timor, stylistically consistent with Tetun art. In Western art, art and religion can be roughly isolated as two discrete areas of experience, but in the Timorese culture these blend into an unfragmented experience. The author leads the reader along the dividing line between the two.

322 **A arte popular em Portugal, vol. 3: ilhas adjecentes e ultramar.** (Folk art in Portugal, vol. 3: adjacent islands and overseas.)
Edited by Fernando de Castro Pires de Lima. Lisbon: Editorial Verbo, 1975. 441p. bibliog.

This general treatise, in a chapter written by Luís Filipe Thomaz, with its murky black-and-white photographs, rather puts down the Timorese artistic tradition by claiming it does not have the 'major' arts – stone architecture, sculpture or painting – only decorative arts. It covers architecture, boat design, and tortoiseshell and bamboo work.

323 **Power and gold: jewellery from Indonesia, Malaysia and the Philippines.**
Susan Rodgers. Geneva: Barbier-Muller Museum, 1985. 369p. maps.
bibliog.
This beautiful catalogue, with photographs by Pierre-Alain Ferrazzini, includes some
pieces from West and Central Timor, mainly from the Atoni. The author runs through
the jewellery and ornaments of Ndao, Roti and, on Timor, the Atoni, the Tetun, the
Makassai and Wehali, noting that the jewellery could bear closer ethnographic
attention as the costumes and ornaments are being converted into dance costumes,
much as Timor princedoms are being fitted into the developing Indonesian nation.
There is also a note on the gold and silversmiths of Ndao.

Architecture

324 **Casa Turi-Sai: um tipo de casa timorense.** (The Turi-Sai house: a type
of Timorese house.)
Jorge Barros. *Garcia de Orta, Série Antropologia*, vol. 2, no. 1–2
(1975), p. 1–34. bibliog.
A description of the structure of the house and the sociomythical and religious
symbolism associated with it.

325 **Arquitectura timorense.** (Timorese architecture.)
Ruy Cinatti, Leopoldo de Almeida, Sousa Mendes. Lisbon: Instituto
de Investigação Científica Tropical/Museu de Etnologia, 1987. 230p.
maps.
This work defines and analyses the principal types of East Timorese habitation and
their relationship with the island's natural and cultural habitat. There is firstly an
introduction to the land, peoples, and means of subsistence in East Timor. The types
of architecture and settlement pattern are then dealt with according to the Portuguese
administrative regions. Each region is introduced by a description of the environment
and people and the whole book is excellently illustrated with numerous photographs
and line drawings. There are also chapters on building materials and techniques and
the architecture of the Portuguese colonial period.

326 **La maison ema (Timor portugais).** (The Ema house [Portuguese
Timor].)
Brigitte Clamagirand. *Asie du Sud-Est et Monde Insulindien*, vol. 6,
no. 2–3, (June–Sept. 1975), p.35–60. map.
Adapted from the author's PhD thesis, this describes the Ema house, home and loft,
its site, internal layout and inventory, giving a journal of the reconstruction of the
lineage house and the different associated rites.

327 **Order in the Atoni house.**
Clark E. Cunningham. *Bijdragen tot de Taal-, Land- en Volkenkunde*, no. 120 (1964), p. 34–68. bibliog.

A revised edition of this is published in *Right and left: essays on dual symbolic classification* Edited by Rodney Needham (Chicago: University of Chicago Press, 1973. p. 204–38). In this well-presented article, illustrated with sketches and diagrams, the author lucidly presents his case that the house may be an effective means to communicate ideas from generation to generation in a preliterate society. In describing each part of the house and its symbolism, he ties the house in with much else of Atoni life.

Textiles and weaving

328 **Le travail du coton chez les Ema de Timor de Timor Portugais.** (The use of cotton among the Ema of Portuguese Timor.)
Brigitte Clamagirand. *Archipel*, no. 3 (1972), p. 55–80.

An excellent introduction to the preparation of cotton and its use in the weaving of textiles, with accompanying diagrams and photographs. There is a detailed guide to spinning the thread and preparing for it for *ikat*: tying the threads, dying and weaving and some of the designs used. The author also points out the social and economic importance of weaving for the Ema.

329 **Handwoven textiles of southeast Asia.**
Sylvia Fraser-Lu. Singapore: Oxford University Press, 1988. 230p. map. bibliog.

This is an essential layperson's introduction, with plenty of diagrams, sketches and colour photographs. Information is given on techniques, history, materials, looms and the symbolism and ritual concerning weaving in southeast Asia as a whole. Its treatment of Timor is fairly slight, but it covers all the main points and has a good bibliography.

330 **Splendid symbols: textiles and tradition in Indonesia.**
Mattiebelle Gittinger. Singapore: Oxford University Press, 1990. p. 174–83. map. bibliog. 240p.

Gittinger describes the regional variations found in textiles throughout West Timor, primarily among the Atoni: between the sexes, the importance of colour, the special costume *pilu saluf* of the headhunters, men's purses that are given to them by their prospective brides. There is also a discussion of the social and ceremonial importance of textiles. The following chapter deals with the islands of Roti and Ndao, whose weaving is similar in their use of warp ikat, muted dye range and a moderate design scale.

331 **Tenun *ikat*; Indonesian *ikats*.**
Suwati Kartiwa, English text by Judi Achjadi.   Jakarta: Djambatan,
1987. 97p. map. bibliog.

Ikat is predominant in Nusa Tenggara Timur, including Timor, and this brief book
gives an account of the development of *ikat* weaving, a background of the communities
producing it, external influences , acculturation of techniques, thread types, design
systems and utilization. It is particularly important for its glossary of terms associated
with *ikat* production.

332 **Die primären Textiltechniken auf Sumba, Rote und Timor.** (Primary
methods of textile manufacture in Sumba, Roti and Timor.)
Irmgard Müller.   PhD thesis, Universität Basel, 1967. map. bibliog.
362p.

Absolutely exhaustive monograph on the physical construction of woven goods, not
only textiles but also basketware, which in these islands can be highly elaborate.
Illustrated throughout with sketches and diagrams and exploded views of the pieces to
allow the reader to see how the pieces are made up.

333 **The weaving and waving of Nusa Tenggara Timur.**
Jes A. Therik.   Jakarta: East Nusa Tenggara Pavilion of the Beautiful
Indonesia in Miniature Park, 1990. 16p. map.

This glossy tourist pamphlet, with parallel Indonesian and English texts, gives a very
brief introduction to weaving, making the point that, to many tourists, the acronym
commonly used for Nusa Tenggara Timur, NTT, means 'nusa tenun tangan': the
islands of handmade weaving. Of particular interest are the pages on Bunak weaving.

Reference Works

334 Amnesty International Report.
Amnesty International Publications, 1975/76–. annual.

This is an annual review of human rights violations worldwide. It covers both Indonesia and East Timor and describes Amnesty's efforts over the previous year. There are appendices regarding missions accomplished, discussions with government authorities, trial observations, research, statutes, full coverage of news releases during the previous year and a guide to the signatory states to selected international human rights treaties. There is a guide to other regional human rights treaties and to the Body of Principles regarding human rights adopted by the United Nations General Assembly in 1988.

335 Asia Yearbook.
Hong Kong: Review Publishing, 1960–. annual.

Compiled by the editors and correspondents of the weekly *Far Eastern Economic Review* (q.v), the *Asia Yearbook* contains valuable up-to-date information on thirty-one Asian–Pacific countries from Afghanistan to New Zealand. Each country is the subject of a separate chapter sub-divided under the headings: 'Politics and social affairs'; 'Foreign relations': and 'Economy and infrastructure', and each is accompanied by a list of current cabinet members and a 'Databox' of essential vital statistics. Prior to the country-by-country survey there are chapters reviewing topics such as finance, investment, commodities and energy from a regional perspective and the yearbook concludes with a 'News roundup', a summation of the past year's main stories.

336 **Indonesian ports: an atlas–gazetteer.**
Gale Dixon.   Townsville, Australia: James Cook University of North
Queensland, 1985. rev. ed. 159p. map. bibliog. (Centre of Southeast
Asian Studies monograph, no. 16).
Despite chopping off some of East Timor (hopefully a part without any major ports)
this is an excellent research aid for those studying inter-island shipping or for those
involved in trade or development in the island. It lists the principal ports on the island
– Kupang, Atapupu, Dili and Tenau, as well as many of the smaller ones, giving
information on draft and length of the wharf (if any), the available port services, pilots,
charts and settlement type. The ports are listed both according to name and also
according to their latitude position.

337 **U.S. Board on Geographic Names: Indonesia.**
Prepared by William R. Garren, Boyd D. Peterson, Carl R. Page.
Washington DC: Defense Mapping Agency, 1982. 3rd ed. 2 vols.
Lists 71,000 names approved by the United States Board on Geographic Names, for
geographic features in Indonesia (including East Timor). The coverage corresponds to
that of maps at the scale of 1:500,000. Entries include names of populated places,
administrative divisions (*propinsi* and *kabupaten*), islands, mountains and other
cultural and physical features. Each name has a description of the feature e.g. town,
river, latitude and longitude, a Universal Transverse Mercator (UTM) Grid Reference
and a sheet number based on the Joint Operations Graphic Series 501, worldwide,
map-sheet numbering scheme.

338 **Indonesia: an official handbook.**
Department of Information.   Jakarta: Republic of Indonesia,
Department of Information. annual.
Annual Indonesian government gazetteer for public release, with statistics and
photographs in a glossy format and information on history, the land and its people,
government and development.

The Indonesian occupation of East Timor, 1974–1989: a chronology.
See item no. 214.

Bibliographies

339 Some Portuguese sources for Indonesian historiography.
Charles Ralph Boxer.   In: *An introduction to Indonesian historiography*. Edited by Soedjatmoko, Mohammad Ali, G.J. Resink, G.McT. Kahin. Ithaca, New York: Cornell University Press, 1965, p. 217–33.

Portugal naturally represents one of the richest veins of material for anyone conducting research into Timorese colonial history. This is a thorough account of all the primary, and some secondary, sources known to this pre-eminent specialist on Timor.

340 Some sources for the history of Timor.
Charles Ralph Boxer.   *Far Eastern Quarterly*, vol. 9, no. 1. (Nov. 1949), p. 63–66.

For those intending to conduct more thorough research into Portuguese Timorese history this is an excellent annotated bibliographical essay of the best Portuguese and some Dutch secondary sources as well as locations of the best collections of primary information.

341 Excerpta Indonesica.
Leiden: Centre for Documentation on Modern Indonesia of the Royal Institute of Linguistics and Anthropology, 1970–. biannual.

Contains abstracts of selected periodical articles published from 1981 and annotations of selected recent books on Indonesia in the fields of the social sciences and humanities.

342 **Bibliography of Indonesian peoples and cultures.**
Raymond Kennedy. New Haven, Connecticut: Yale University Press,
1974. 3rd ed. (Yale Anthropological Studies no. 4). Revised by Thomas
W. Maretzki and H.T. Fischer. Human Relations Area Files,
Behaviour Science Bibliographies, 1962. 207p.
This contains more than 200 references to Timor and Roti (p. 180–82), being especially
strong on older Dutch references to West Timor, but it is neither annotated nor
selective.

343 **Contribution to a bibliography of the Timor crisis: material in the
Australian National University library.**
George Miller. In: *Southeast Asian Research Materials Group
Newsletter*, no. 9 (Oct. 1977), p. 4–7.
Australia represents one of the best sources of reference material on Timor and the
Australian National University has one of the best academic collections of the more
obscure materials – publications from action groups on Timor, publications from
Timor, newspapers and other secondary material.

344 **A propos de quelques livres recents sur le Timor Oriental.** (Some recent
books on East Timor.)
René Pélissier. *Afrique et l'Asie Modernes*, no. 133 (1982), p. 54–62.
Examines several recent books on the former Portuguese colony on the island of
Timor, including bibliographies, scientific, sociological and political books, as well as
some newspaper articles.

345 **Du Sahara à Timor: 700 livres analysés (1980–1990) sur l'Afrique et
l'Insulinde ex-ibériques.** (From the Sahara to Timor: an analysis of 700
books [1980–1990] on ex-Iberian possessions in Africa and the
Indonesian archipelago.)
René Pélissier. Orgeval, France: Pélissier, 1991. 350p.
This bibliographic essay covers a total of forty-four books, articles, pamphlets,
conference papers and government documents in English, French, Portuguese and
Spanish, starting from the start of the conflict in 1974.

346 **A bibliography of Timor.**
Kevin Sherlock. Canberra: Australian National University,
Research School of Pacific Studies, 1980. 292p. map. (Aids to Research
Series, no. A/4).
Compiled to cover all aspects of Timor and Roti this is the best starting point for
research of any type. Focusing generally on Western language sources, it is of
particular use for details of unpublished works relating to development, and the
Indonesian invasion of East Timor. There is only an author index and the references
are not annotated.

347 **Timor during the first and second world wars: some notes on sources.**
Kevin Sherlock. *Kabar Seberang*, no. 19–20 (1988), p. 41–56.

This bibliographic essay includes all the references, both seen and unseen and in all languages known to the author at that time. The section on the Second World War has a separate part devoted to books of personal experiences, and there is a guide to some of the Portuguese and Timorese people mentioned in C.C.H. Wray's book *Timor 1942: Australian commandos at war with the Japanese* (q.v.).

348 **A further contribution to a bibliography on East Timor: a multi-media survey, 1975–1978.**
William Tully. In: *Southeast Asian Research Materials Group, Newsletter*, no. 11 (Oct. 1978), p. 3–10.

A selected and annotated bibliography of fifty items intended to add to Miller's bibliography of 1977, and anticipating Sherlock's of 1980. Includes maps, discs, tapes, films and radio transcripts to supplement the more conventional material. There is an emphasis on political, economic, cultural and sociological writings surrounding the Indonesian invasion.

Periodicals

349 **Asian Thought and Society: An International Review.**
New York: New York State University, 1976–. 3 times a year.
Contains international specialist contributions in English on a whole range of Asian subjects, including book reviews. Materials on Timorese related affairs appear regularly.

350 **Asiaweek.**
Hong Kong: Asiaweek, 1975–. weekly.
Equivalent of *Time* or *Newsweek* for all of Asia. News and in-depth reports on politics, economics, social affairs and culture. Editorials and literary reviews reflect a definite Asian point of view.

351 **East Timor News.**
Lisbon: Peace is Possible in East Timor, Committee for the Rights of the Maubere People, 1987–. monthly.
Analyses of news coverage of East Timor in the Portuguese press, and details of events concerned with East Timor in the international arena.

352 **Em Timor-Leste, a Paz é Possivél.** (Peace is Possible in East Timor.)
Lisbon: Peace is Possible in East Timor, 1982–. bi-monthly.
This publication has access to sources in the East Timorese church and is regularly produced in issues concerning particular subjects.

353 **Far Eastern Economic Review.**
Hong Kong: Far Eastern Economic Review, 1946–. weekly.
A valuable source of material on political and economic affairs of the Far East, including articles, statistical surveys and special numbers. Indonesian affairs form part of its regular coverage.

Periodicals

354 Indonesia Reports.
Lanham-Seabrook, Maryland: News Bulletin of Indonesia Publications.

Indonesia Reports covers politics, human rights, culture and society, business and economy, documenting and interpreting current events and research on Indonesia for those in government, business, the media, NGOs and higher education. The same organization also publishes *Indonesia News Service* which is a more up-to-date version of the 'log' section of *Indonesia Reports*, appearing one to three times weekly, and the newsletters *Indonesia Issues* and *Indonesia Mirror*, which present interpretive essays on a wide range of subjects. See also *Inside Indonesia: Bulletin of the Indonesian Resources and Information Programme (IRIP)* (1984. quarterly). Written by academic specialists, members of overseas and agencies, development action groups and trade unions, this journal discusses Indonesian current affairs and development issues. East and West Timor are widely covered.

355 Journal of Contemporary Asia.
Stockholm: Journal of Contemporary Asia, 1970–. quarterly.

A scholarly international quarterly devoted to Asian economic, political and social problems and conditions. The journal is left-leaning and has a sympathetic attitude toward emerging Asian nations.

356 Summary of World Broadcasts. Part 3 – Far East.
Caversham Park, England: Monitoring Service of the British Broadcasting Corporation, 1949–. daily.

An invaluable publication for journalists and others who need to keep track of contemporary events as they unfold, this provides a selection of edited extracts from Far Eastern radio broadcasts, press articles and official reports. Equally useful is the equivalent United States publication *FBIS Daily Report: East Asia* (Springfield, Virginia: National Technical Information service, 1974–. daily), a less up-to-date selection from which is published periodically under the title *JPRS Report: East Asia – Southeast Asia* (Arlington, Virginia: Joint Publications Reasearch Services, 1979–).

357 Tapol Bulletin.
London: Indonesian Human Rights Campaign, 1973–. bimonthly.

Regularly covers events in East Timor, particularly as they relate to Indonesian politics. Tapol also publishes irregular reports, those of potential interest are: no. 2, *Joint statement by Union of Democratic Timorese–Fretilin, March 1986*; no. 5, *The 1983 Indonesian election in East Timor*; no. 14, *United Nations resolutions on East Timor, 1975–1982*; no. 17, *The killing fields of East Timor*. The last report gathers together comment and analysis in the British press of the killings of mourners by Indonesian soldiers on 12 November 1991 at the Santa Cruz church in Dili.

358   **Timor Informations.**
Paris: Association de Solidarité avec Timor Oriental, 1975–. irregular.
The bulletin of the French East Timor Committee, focusing on national and international diplomacy.

359   **Timor Link.**
London: Catholic Institute for International Relations, 1985–.
quarterly.
Recently relaunched after a publishing hiatus since 1988, this uses church sources in East Timor and Indonesia.

Index

The index is a single alphabetical sequence of authors (personal and corporate), titles of publications and subjects. Index entries refer to both the main items and to other works mentioned in the note to each item. Title entries are in italics. Numbers refer to bibliographic entries.

Maps of Timor

These maps show the more important towns and other features.

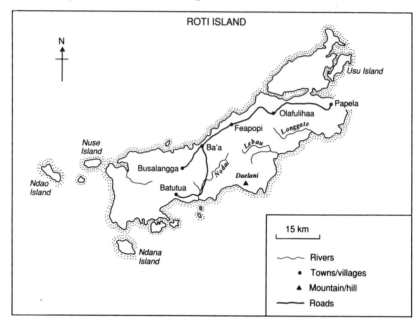

ROTI ISLAND

N

Usu Island

Papela

Olafulihaa

Feapopi

Longgate

Nuse Island

Ba'a

Lebau

Busalangga

Nodai

Daelani

Batutua

Ndao Island

Ndana Island

15 km

~~~ Rivers
• Towns/villages
▲ Mountain/hill
— Roads

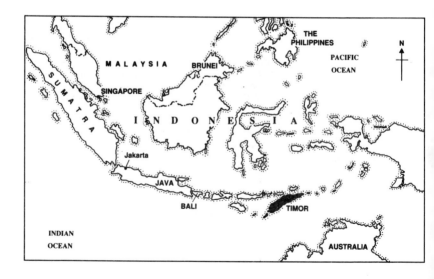

THE PHILIPPINES

N

MALAYSIA

BRUNEI

PACIFIC OCEAN

SINGAPORE

SUMATRA

I N D O N E S I A

Jakarta

JAVA

BALI

TIMOR

INDIAN OCEAN

AUSTRALIA

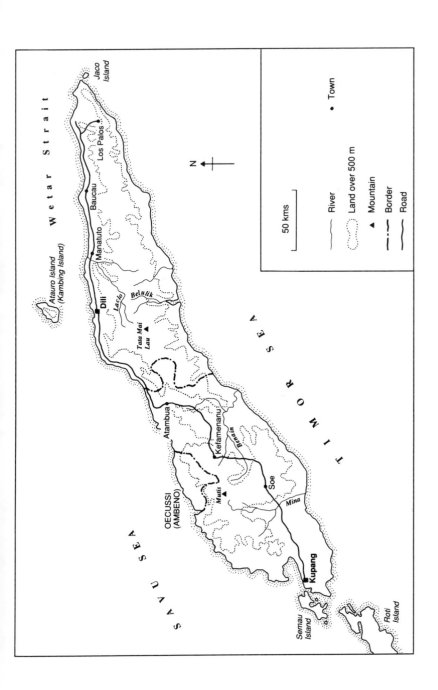